MOTHERING THE MOTHER

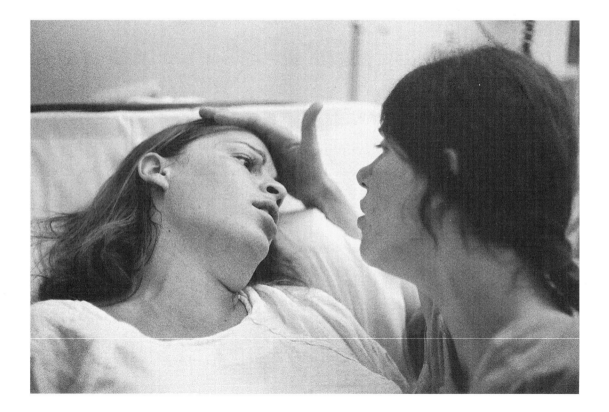

. . .

MOTHERING THE MOTHER

. . .

How a Doula Can Help You Have a Shorter, Easier, and Healthier Birth

. . .

MARSHALL H. KLAUS, M.D.

JOHN H. KENNELL, M.D.

PHYLLIS H. KLAUS, M.Ed., C.S.W.

Photographs by Suzanne Arms

A MERLOYD LAWRENCE BOOK

ADDISON-WESLEY PUBLISHING COMPANY
Reading, Massachusetts   Menlo Park, California   New York
Don Mills, Ontario   Wokingham, England   Amsterdam   Bonn
Sydney   Singapore   Tokyo   Madrid   San Juan
Paris   Seoul   Milan   Mexico City   Taipei

All photographs are by Suzanne Arms, except those by Marshall Klaus on pages 95, 96, 100, 103, 105, and 106, and by Lauren Daniel on page 42.

Many of the designations used by manufacturers and sellers to distinguish their products are claimed as trademarks. Where those designations appear in this book and Addison-Wesley was aware of a trademark claim, the designations have been printed in initial capital letters.

Library of Congress Cataloging-in-Publication Data

Klaus, Marshall H., 1927–
    Mothering the mother : how a doula can help you have a shorter, easier, and healthier birth / Marshall H. Klaus, John H. Kennell, Phyllis H. Klaus ; photographs by Suzanne Arms.
      p.   cm.
    "A Merloyd Lawrence book."
    Includes bibliographical references and index.
    ISBN 0-201-56797-0. — ISBN 0-201-63272-1 (pbk.)
    1. Doulas. 2. Natural childbirth—Coaching. I. Kennell, John H., 1922– . II. Klaus, Phyllis H. III. Title.
RG950.K56 1993
618.4'5—dc20   92-35509
                                         CIP

Cover photographs by Suzanne Arms
Cover design by Diana Coe
Copy edited by Sharon Sharp
Text design by Karen Savary
Set in 12-point Bembo by Shepard Poorman

56789-VB-0099989796
Fifth printing, September 1996

. . .

DEDICATION

We dedicate this book to all the sensitive and caring women who have provided continuous support during labor for the mothers in our studies. They have helped us in immeasurable ways to evaluate, describe, and begin to understand the power of their presence. We also dedicate this book to all the doulas in the future who will enable mothers and their partners to have a less complicated and more rewarding birth.

. . .

ACKNOWLEDGMENTS

Our understanding of the needs of mothers during labor developed over the last fifteen years during our systematic studies. Insights also came from discussions with doulas and with close colleagues Steven Robertson, Susan McGrath, Roberto Sosa, Manuel de Carvalho, Larry Olsen, and Clark Hinkley. We also thank the medical students, and especially Wendy Freed, who eighteen years ago sparked our interest in exploring the needs of women during labor through observations she made when she stayed with ten mothers during labor as part of another study. Apparently benefiting from her supportive presence, these mothers all had a remarkably short labor and a complication-free birth. This observation was a critical stimulus to our exploration of the effects of a doula.

After reading early drafts of the book, the perceptive comments of Susan and Bob Sholtes, Laura and David Abada, Nanette and Mark Linderman, Majeed Al-Mateen and his wife, Lillian Koblenz, Sharon Ledbetter, David Beguin, and Roberta O'Bell were especially helpful.

We appreciate the guidance of Dr. Peter Boylan in understanding the Active Management of Labor and observing the birthing process at the National

Maternity Hospital in Dublin, Ireland. Special thanks to Madeleine Shearer, Claudia Lowe, and Wendy Roope, who provided unique criticism. We thank our secretaries for their excellent work and patience: in Cleveland, Dorise Hunter and Dianne Kodger, and in Oakland, Terri Brown. Of course we thank Peggy Kennell for her early contributions and her strong, doula-like patience and support.

Finally, our heartfelt thanks to Merloyd Lawrence for her continuing encouragement, sensitive understanding, and remarkable editing skills.

. . .

DOULA

Doula is a Greek word referring to an experienced woman who helps other women. The word has now come to mean a woman experienced in childbirth who provides continuous physical, emotional, and informational support to the mother before, during, and just after childbirth.

CONTENTS

1
· · ·
THE NEED FOR SUPPORT IN LABOR
· · ·

The family is born in the delivery room.
JOHNNY LIND, M.D.
Stockholm

· · · WOMEN HELPING WOMEN in labor is an ancient and widespread practice. For instance, according to anthropological data that we reviewed for 128 nonindustrialized hunting and gathering and agricultural societies, all but one offered mothers continuous support during labor and delivery. As childbirth moved from home to hospital, however, and became safer for mothers whose conditions put them at risk, this vital ingredient in childbirth began to disappear. While efforts to involve fathers and to introduce other humane practices into hospital births have done much to improve this situation, an important link remains missing. Childbirth is now lonelier and more psychological-ly stressful. For some mothers, left to labor largely on their own, birth becomes "solitary confinement."

In the past fifteen years, together with colleagues, we have studied the effects of restoring to the childbirth experience this important element of having women as helpers during labor. Continuous support from an experienced labor companion has proven dramatically beneficial. In studies of over 1,500 women involving comparisons of outcomes with and without such support, we have seen a major reduction in the length of labor, a greater than 50 percent drop in cesarean sections, a remarkable drop in the mothers' need for pain medication, and several other important and measurable benefits, which we describe in the chapters that follow.

The continuous support was provided by caring, experienced women we call *doulas.* In searching for a term to describe this role, we wanted a word with a nonmedical connotation that would stress the value of a woman companion as attentive and comforting. We turned to the Greek word *doula,* meaning "woman caregiver." Our first exposure to the word came from Dana Raphael's use of the term to describe "one or more individuals, often female, who give psychological encouragement and physical assistance to the newly delivered mother."[33] We use the word in the now widely accepted sense of an experienced labor companion who provides the woman and her partner both emotional and physical support throughout the entire labor and delivery, and to some extent, afterward. Other people use terms such as *labor coach, monitrice,* or *childbirth assistant.* Whatever the term, we hope our readers will come away with an understanding of the vital shared ingredient that makes this role so powerful and beneficial.

In this book we describe what a doula can provide, both during and immediately after birth, and how she is trained. We discuss the results of our studies on labor outcomes and differentiate not only between the assistance of a doula and the equally vital help of fathers but also between the work of the doula and that of the nurse, physician, or midwife. We also describe the experience with doulas in other parts of the world, offer guidance in finding and evaluating a doula, and give in Appendix A information on how a doula is trained.

We realize that a woman delivering a baby may be married or single and accompanied by the father, her own mother, or a close friend. When we use words such as *father, partner, couple,* and *parents,* we mean to include all types of family arrangements. Also, for simplicity, we use the words *mother* and *father,* rather than *mother-to-be* and *father-to-be,* for a woman and man as they share in the experience of labor and delivery.

TYPES OF LABOR SUPPORT

When embarking on one of the most meaningful experiences of their lives—expecting their first baby—a couple fantasizes about what the labor and delivery will be like. They may have a dream of how it will be—perhaps hoping that this pregnancy and birth will be all their own, something they do together without anyone else's interference. At the same time, they will have fears. On the one hand, they may picture being alone together, with the father being the main helper and support, and music playing in the background as they go through labor without interruptions or interventions and then have idyllic quiet time with their new baby. On the other hand, they may worry about pain, loss of control, problems for the baby, or life-threatening complications.

Given these hopes and fears, all mothers and fathers need emotional support and help during labor. Much of this support they can provide to each other. The mother needs to feel the father's caring, love, sense of connection, responsibility, and sense of sharing in the intimate experience of bringing their child into the world. The father or other chosen partner has a strong desire to help, to participate, to feel useful and active, and to feel important and necessary for the mother.

But when two people share an emotional bond and an ongoing relationship, it is very difficult for that companion to remain continuously objective, calm, and removed to some degree from the mother's discomfort, fears, or dangers. In most cases—and this cannot be stated too often—the father will have the unexpressed but deeply felt question, Will everything be all right? Also, a father often has had little or no experience with the birth process.

For these reasons, every woman in labor needs not only the father or other chosen partner but also a nurturing, experienced person—a doula—who can calmly and skillfully help her cope with labor and be a reassuring and constant presence for both her and the father. The doula gives a level of support different from that of a person who is intimately related to the woman in labor.

These two kinds of support complement each other. A doula can help a woman work with her labor and guide her on how to stay relaxed and comfortable at home until labor is well established. Prenatally, the doula can show the pregnant woman how she will have the ability and confidence to be an advocate on her own behalf. In the hospital the doula can help the father or other partner be less anxious. With her practiced skill, the doula serves as a role model for the less experienced person.

Very often the couple worry that an outside support person will take over and control the labor experience, as many individuals providing labor assistance have traditionally done. The training of a doula is quite different, emphasizing quiet reassurance and enhancement of the natural abilities of the laboring woman. A doula is constantly aware that the couple will carry the memory of this experience throughout their lives. As we discuss in Chapters 4, 5, and 6, the doula is there to help the parents have the type of birthing experience they want.

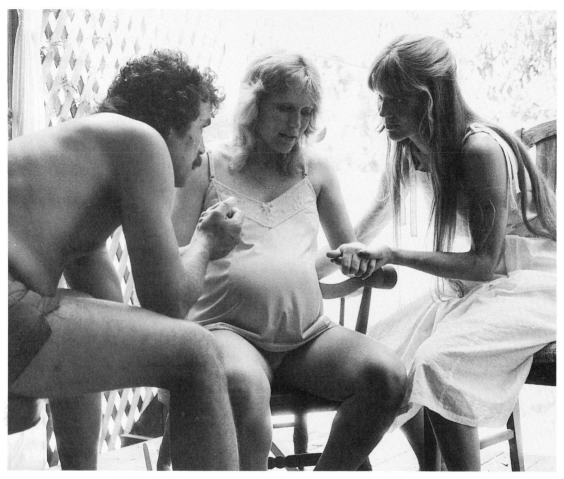

Early labor at home on the porch with the support of the father and doula.

For millennia the relationship of mother to daughter, of older experienced woman to younger birthing woman, was respected and understood. Today, although many woman may want their own mothers' help during labor, most of today's grandmothers are not experienced around birth. The experience of women who gave birth in the 1950s and 1960s may not have been ideal. Also, many women are distant from their adult daughters geographically and some, psychologically. Many expectant women today prefer not to have their mothers at the actual birth, even if they have a caring relationship. Many expectant women prefer to have the father present, and it is often easier for the couple to have a nonrelated but caring person help them. Sometimes men who have become involved in birth through childbirth courses may feel their position is usurped if their mother-in-law or a close friend of the mother's is acting as the main support during labor. However, laboring women's mothers and friends can be important support people along with the fathers. The doula role is designed to provide a nurturing, helpful, and objective female supporter so that the family member chosen to be present does not have sole responsibility for the labor. It is not an attempt to interfere with the relationship between the woman and her partner or other family member.

THE NEEDS OF FATHERS DURING LABOR AND DELIVERY

In asking fathers to be the main support, our society may have created a very difficult expectation for them to meet. This is like asking fathers to play in a professional football game after several lectures but without any training or practice games. Couples sometimes get the mistaken impression from childbirth classes that by using a number of simple exercises, the father can be a main source of support and knowledge for the entire labor when the nurse is unavailable. This is true for a small number of fathers, but most fathers—especially first-time ones—do not get enough opportunity in the classes to observe and practice. Often the dilemma for childbirth instructors is how to get fathers to be more a part of the experience and appreciate what actually lies ahead. Fathers entering into this new role often feel nervous, joke frequently, and consciously or unconsciously wonder about their place in this whole obstetrical arena. Dr. Martin Greenberg, an experienced physician who has done research with new fathers, commented: "I didn't realize until later how frightened and angry I felt at the staff for being left alone with my wife when having our first baby."

In no other area of the hospital is a family member asked to take on such a significant caretaking role as in childbirth. When working in the obstetrical unit, we have often been struck by how terribly relieved fathers are when an experienced nurse or midwife enters the room and remains with them. This feeling of relief enables the fathers to be much more relaxed, loving, and emotionally available than when they bear the burden of responsibility alone.

We therefore want to protect the father's need to be present *at his own comfort level* and his right to be emotionally connected to his partner and child. Few fathers want to be—or should be—the sole support person in the room. As we discuss in Chapter 5, the mother gains more assured, steady emotional support from her partner if he is less worried about what he is supposed to do and if they both can relax and trust the doula's expert care. As one father noted: "I've run a number of marathons, I've done a lot of hiking with a heavy backpack, and I've worked for forty hours straight on-call; but going through labor with my wife was more strenuous and exhausting than any of these other experiences. We could never have done it without the doula. She was crucial for us." His wife added: "I want the doula there to assure me that everything is fine and to comfort me. I want my husband there for emotional support."

A laboring woman's rapid changes of mood may alarm an inexperienced father and compound the mother's fears. "If you leave the mother alone for even five minutes," a doula commented to us, "she begins to become distressed. She begins to fall apart and lose control, and when you return, it may take a half hour to get her settled down." Fathers express feelings of mounting anxiety. Underlying this anxiety is often an unexpressed fear of danger for the mother or child, as well as distress for the mother's pain. Although fathers have many positive feelings and great anticipation, these nega-tive feelings can get in the way and, in turn, affect the progress of the labor itself. Over and over again we have been impressed by the calming influence the doula has for both the mother and father as she explains what is happening, uses her extensive experience to help the mother, and supports the parents in having the kind of experience they original-ly desired.

A VARIETY OF SETTINGS FOR BIRTH

Hospitals and obstetric caregivers, including physicians, nurses, and mid-wives, approach delivery from very different perspectives. The role of a doula or other provider of labor support will be affected by these differences. On one end of the spectrum, childbirth is viewed as a normal physiological event that follows a natural course. Interventions needed for

A mother and her doula late in labor.

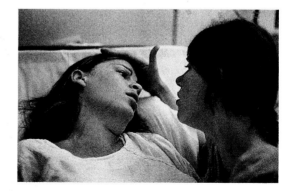

these natural deliveries are seen as minor, although the personnel must remain alert for any medical sign of complications. On the other end of this spectrum, childbirth is a medical event fraught with potential danger. The comparison below shows some of the differences in the two approaches.

In planning or thinking about their own delivery, expectant parents should know about the different practices of the physicians and midwives in their community. By knowing which approaches these professionals tend to adopt, they

TWO VIEWS OF CHILDBIRTH

NATURAL	*MEDICAL*
Mother stays home as long as possible	Mother comes to hospital shortly after labor begins
Mother walking around, taking liquids orally	Mother in bed with an I.V.
Monitored every fifteen minutes with a stethoscope; fetal monitor when medically indicated	Continuous electronic fetal monitoring throughout labor for every mother
Mother encouraged to choose positions of comfort and to walk to stimulate labor	Mother remains in bed; medication and rupturing of membranes used to stimulate labor
Father encouraged to be present along with an experienced labor companion (doula)	Father present, but the couple otherwise alone between nurses' and physician's visits to check on progress of labor
Upright or other gravity-assisted positions for birth	Lying-on-back position with legs in stirrups for birth
The baby eased out, without an episiotomy	Routine episiotomy for delivery of head
Babies stay with mother and father for extended contact after birth	Short period of contact for mother and baby; baby taken to nursery

·   ·   ·

can make a more informed choice in order to meet the mother's medical, emotional, and physical needs.

PRESSURES ON THE HOSPITAL STAFF

Many people do not appreciate that an obstetrical staff of nurses and doctors provides care for a wide range of patients. In the United States, ninety-five percent of deliveries are normal and routine, but 5 to 10 percent require an intensive effort with the use of advanced technology, consultants, and additional ancillary personnel. When the special cases arise, this reduces the number of nurses available to work with the larger group of mothers who are having routine, normal deliveries. In addition, the numerous cesarean sections in most hospitals also tie up the nursing personnel.

Studies by Ellen Hodnett in Toronto noted that women planning a hospital birth rarely expected to have a nurse with them throughout labor.[10] The women usually felt the nurses would be busy or viewed their role as purely technical. She commented, "Recognizing that laboring women require psychological support and realizing that nurses have little time to give it, hospitals have increasingly permitted and encouraged husbands to assume active roles in the care of their wives during labor." In addition, in hospitals many different

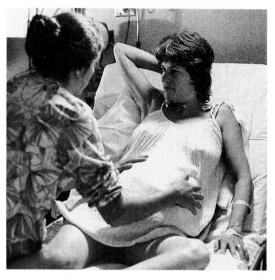

The mother and doula begin their work.

caregivers are often involved with one mother. A recent study found that women giving birth encountered an average of 6.4 unfamiliar professionals during labor. The presence of many strangers can disrupt the labor and confuse the mother.

At home and in some hospitals, midwives who care for only one mother at a time, continuously attending each from early labor on, meet both the medical and emotional needs of the mother and father. When a hospital or other birth setting provides such continuous one-to-one nursing or one-to-one midwifery care and that caregiver's goal is to reassure, relax, comfort, and inform the mother rather than to tend only to the needed medical interventions, that person takes the same supportive role as a doula. Many nurses who care deeply for the emotional as well as the physical well-being of their childbearing patients are happy when they can provide such uninterrupted care.

In most cases, however, nurses on the delivery floor and hospital-based midwives generally care for several patients at one time, monitoring the progress of labor; the vital signs of the mother, such as heart rate, blood pressure, and temperature; and fetal well-being, with heart-rate changes. In non-high-risk situations obstetricians and family physicians are not in constant attendance but

The doula uses her touch to support this mother, who is focusing on breathing slowly and evenly through a contraction.

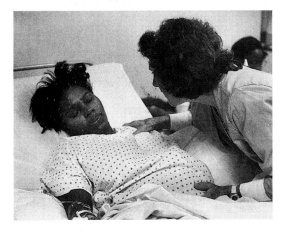

check in and out until late labor. Then they manage the delivery and attend to any medical aspects, giving strong support when they are present.

Many parents expect to handle childbirth alone, but within the circle of a "safe" hospital setting where help is just outside the door. Many nurses believe they should not interfere with the couple's labor and instead, just come in to check on how things are going. When they or the physician come in only intermittently, they may not always recognize the great need that parents have for information and reassurance. It may be difficult for the father to ask for help or to realize when or what type of assistance his wife needs at each stage of labor. He may be getting anxious, and he will often think of "help" only as a medical intervention rather than as assistance with the emotional needs of the mother as she works through contractions. The myth is that the medical caregiver will be continuously present; the reality is almost always different. On most busy obstetric services constant support is not possible.

Two widely respected, experienced, and caring teachers of obstetrics, Drs. Kierin O'Driscoll and Declan Meagher, whose work in Dublin is described in Chapter 7, have recognized the negative effects that a lack of support has on women in labor. When a woman does not have an experienced person to give her continuous personal attention throughout labor and when the father is uncertain, fearful, or becoming anxious himself, they note, "the scenario for many can be written in advance: the woman becomes progressively withdrawn from contact with her surroundings, closes her eyes and buries her face in the pillow, only later to become increasingly active, with contorted features and restless movements, interrupted by outbursts, until finally a state of panic is reached and self control is lost."[31] In our studies we have encountered several occasions in which couples who were reluctant initially to have a supportive companion because they wanted to be alone for this significant event changed their minds completely

The mother, supported by the father and doula, just before delivery (a vaginal birth after cesarean—VBAC).

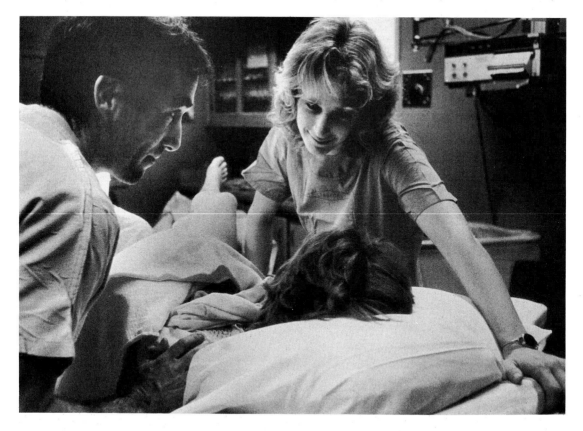

in midlabor and pleaded with us to supply them with a doula.

Chapter 9 offers guidelines on how to find and evaluate a doula. The role of a doula is still being refined, and as we said earlier, labor support can be offered by several other types of professionals. In Appendix A we describe the basic ingredients of doula training.

Our studies have led us to the firm conviction that a doula—a person providing unobtrusive, compassionate, and experienced support throughout labor—is needed by every couple during the delivery of their child. With such help, parents can capture the special moments and priceless experience of their own unique childbirth. This in turn becomes the foundation for strong attachment as the new family comes into being.

2

· · ·

THE DOULA

· · ·

We form such a rapport that a woman
can ask anything of me.

A DOULA

· · · TO UNDERSTAND THE SPE-cial role of a doula, we must first distinguish it from that of the others involved in childbirth. A doula is not a doctor, a nurse, or a midwife. She is not trained to make any medical decisions. However, her training includes learning about the usual medical interventions so that she can explain them to parents in order to relieve some of their uncertainties and anxieties. As an example, fetal monitors may record a very low heart rate (1 to 2 beats per minute) for a few seconds, even though the actual heart rate is a normal 148 beats per minutes. The doula who is knowledgeable about this phenomenon can reassure the mother that the low reading is a problem of the machine, not the baby.

A nurse or midwife can provide support in labor if she does not have other duties, time constraints, or other patients. Many nurses and midwives choose obstetric work because of their empathic interest in helping women during childbirth. But as we saw earlier, the demands of the labor and delivery service, hectic schedules, and a large number of laboring women make it extremely unlikely that nurses or midwives can be totally and continuously available to any one laboring woman for her entire labor.

Some hospitals have birth centers

with one-on-one midwife assignments, but this is not common. Much more often midwives are expected to care for two or more mothers at the same time. When that is the case, they generally welcome the presence of a doula when they have to leave one mother alone to care for another.

It is assumed that a doula will be a woman, and several advantages probably account for this. A mother in labor can usually be less inhibited in the presence of another woman. The intimate aspects of bodily function are more easily expressed with a person of the same gender. In addition, the softer, quieter, gentler, sensitive, nurturing qualities of "mothering" have traditionally come from women in our culture.

Most doulas have delivered children of their own. A woman who has given birth has an innate sense of what the experience is like and provides a natural empathy. However, personal birthing experience is not essential. A number of women who have not been mothers themselves work very sensitively as doulas. Although they do not have firsthand experience of birth, they relate to the birthing woman through their inherent psychological and biological kinship as women.

Unlike many "labor coaches," doulas do not prescribe any set breathing pattern or labor regimen. Instead of the patterned and instructed breathing techniques that have been strongly emphasized in Lamaze training, doulas create an emotional "holding" environment for the mother, encouraging her to allow her own body to tell her what may be best at various times during labor. The doulas cooperate fully with any breathing pattern the couple is prepared to use.

In the following four chapters we describe a doula's actual work. In the next section, we examine the basic nature of her work.

THE DOULA'S ROLE

What does the doula actually do to help the mother? Ideally, her role begins when the doula has an opportunity to meet the mother and the mother's partner one and a half to three months before labor begins—that is, during the third trimester of pregnancy. At that time the doula can learn in detail what the woman or couple expects and wants during labor. She can also find out what the mother has found helpful when feeling tense in other situations and what kinds of soothing make her feel more relaxed or less anxious. For example, a mother may say, "I often feel very relaxed if somebody rubs my shoulders or back very softly and slowly." Then during labor the doula will try this and ask the woman if she finds it helpful.

A doula learns that she has to be willing to take anything for an answer and not be embarrassed or feel foolish. Sometimes an action a woman enjoyed before may not feel right or helpful during the actual labor. The experienced doula develops enough confidence and self-esteem that she is not offended by the woman's seeming rejection of that action. A woman cannot or may not always tell the doula what she likes. Sometimes the doula tries something for a short while, observes the woman, and "reads" her responses. A woman in labor may feel that she must perform and act in a certain way in front of her husband, mother, or mother-in-law. In contrast, the woman can be completely at ease with the doula and unconcerned about having to try to please her or put on a show for her.

This initial visit of the doula with the couple or the pregnant woman becomes a time to build rapport, and it allows the doula to learn what goals and wishes the parents have for the birth of their child. When the expectations are unrealistic, the doula will tactfully explain what she can and cannot do. Two or three visits of the doula with the mother and her partner during pregnancy will allow the relationship to develop. In some cases, these prenatal visits cannot always be arranged. When the doula must first meet the mother at the time of her admission to the hospital, the early period of labor usually allows time for the relationship to proceed.

The most important assurance that a doula can give in these initial visits is that she will remain with the mother throughout the entire labor and not leave her alone. If the doula has to leave to eat or go to the bathroom, she will have the father or nurse stand by for her. The relationship builds on this assurance; it makes the woman and family feel cared for, not alone.

For women in labor much of the birth process is about permission: feeling total permission to be themselves and feeling free to let down emotional and physical barriers and to release expectations— those yardsticks or measures of performance that women carry with them into the institutional environment. Feeling completely safe with another human being creates a kind of freedom that enables a woman to begin to test the limits of her own capacities and to experience capacities possibly not recognized before—or perhaps recognized but not risked. This freedom to be one's true self produces feeling of empowerment, of creativity. As a new mother said to one doula, "Your staying with me all the time and your total support, at the same time trusting me completely, gave me a sense of knowing that I was strong enough to handle anything in my life."

Nadia, an experienced doula, explains that mothers whom she first meets at the hospital are often out of control at the beginning of labor when they first start to experience pain. With each one Nadia asks whether she is afraid, and the mother usually says yes. The doula sees in the mother's face a growing fear about not being able to stand the pain. She explains to the woman that the labor is a very natural process and a natural function of the body. Nadia tells the mother just to let her body do what it has to do. If the mother continues to be scared, Nadia says, "Don't be frightened. Remember to let your breath go through—let it go through. Just breathe it through quietly, and try as much as you can to be relaxed. That's it you see, that's the only thing you have to do." Usually when Nadia quietly and calmly repeats one of these phrases over and over again in a cadence, the mother becomes quiet and peaceful. During this process she begins to feel confidence in herself and in the naturalness of the process.

Another doula, Joyce, describes a different part of her role. In early labor she finds that she gains the confidence of the mother by being cheerful and friendly. She notes that this can be an enjoyable stage, as they get to know each other. This is especially important when the doula and the mother have not met before labor.

As labor progresses, doulas frequently cradle or hold the women in their arms. If a woman should cry, the doula may get a damp cloth and wipe her face. Regardless of the response of the mother to labor, a doula remains encouraging, never trying to discipline the parents and never putting the mother down.

When women experience back labor, a doula suggests a variety of methods to help relieve the discomfort—back rubs, hot cloths, pressure against the back, or sometimes no touch whatsoever. Each mother has differing needs. As labor progresses, the doula asks what the woman would like, and the mother responds. "We form such a rapport that a woman can ask anything of me" said one doula. By her presence, manner, and comforting touch, the doula creates calmness and the essence of relaxation.

In midlabor, as dilatation of the cervical opening increases from five to seven centimeters and labor pains become more frequent and painful, the doula becomes more supportive. At this time the woman's partner may become frightened and also need support and explanations from the doula. It is here that the doula's ability to encourage and verbalize what is happening is deeply reassuring. One father stated after delivery that when the doula said the bloody show was "good, good!" he felt very relieved. "You could never say that enough. It was so helpful."

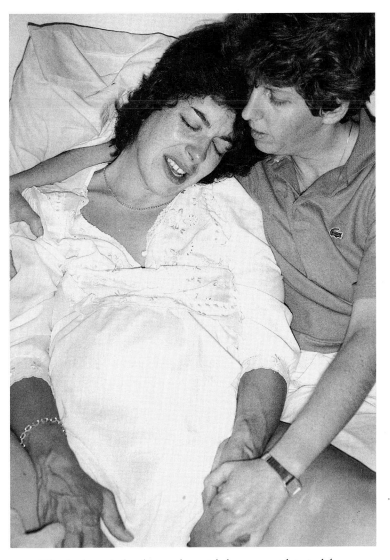

The doula encircles this mother with her support late in labor.

As labor become more intense, the father may move slightly farther away from the woman. If this happens, the doula can move closer or encourage more closeness from the father, if appropriate. At this time the doula continues to reassure the mother and the partner that the labor is progressing normally.

She stays on top of what is happening, explaining each stage and praising the woman about her excellent progress. It is not unusual for some women to ask the doula over and over again when and if she is leaving. When replying, the doula knows it is wise to offer reassurance that she will not leave the mother except perhaps for a few minutes to go to the bathroom.

For the actual delivery, the medical caregivers are in charge. The doula remains by the mother's side along with the father, and afterwards congratulates the parents and especially the new mother on her accomplishment. Even more important is her memory of the couple's prenatal wishes, making certain, for example, that mother and father have time alone with the baby and the mother breast-feeds early.

When the doula visits with the family the day after the delivery, she asks them what they remember about the birth and if they have any questions or concerns. The doula spends time discussing the birth experience, allowing the parents to share all their positive feelings and, if appropriate, their negative feelings. The doula encourages them to talk, and she can add what was forgotten. Almost all mothers gain from hearing the details that fill in many of the missing pieces of the experience for them. From this they gain a new perception of their own participation. Often mothers feel they failed to perform well and did not do something right. This retelling of the birth story helps them understand what actually went on during their labor and delivery. It is an opportunity to heighten the mother's self-image by pointing out the strength she showed and the way her body followed its age-old biological course. If there were complications, the doula helps the mother integrate and sometimes reframe the experience.

THE DOULA AND THE HOSPITAL STAFF

A doula's efforts are more effective when she is known and respected by the personnel on the delivery floor and other hospital staff. The laboring mother has a vastly different experience when the doula has worked with the same staff repeatedly, in contrast to when a stranger is working as a doula. The more knowledgeable the doula is about the unit, the more helpful she can be to the parents. The better the staff know the doula, the more likely they are to be supportive to her. Whenever possible, it is desirable for doulas to be familiar with, and in turn to be recognized and appreciated by, the staff at two or three hospitals in the community that her families use for childbirth. She may receive her training in one hospital but work regularly in several others.

A doula's success also depends on her ability to get along with a diverse group of hospital staff members. In a receptive situation, her ability to become closely connected to the woman in labor, to pick up the woman's signals and calm her, can often shift a potentially difficult situation into one that is easily managed. Once they have seen a doula have this effect, nurses are generally delighted to have her on the labor and delivery floor. Physicians also recognize her value and respect her.

In advance of any work at a particular hospital, the doula will want to introduce herself to the labor and delivery floor, meet the head nurse and other personnel, and learn about the routines for labor, delivery, and the postpartum period. When you work in somebody else's kitchen, you need to know where they keep the flour and sugar and how they wash the dishes. Similarly it is also important to know the admitting and labor and delivery practices unique to a particular obstetrical unit so the doula can ease the transition from home to car to hospital for laboring women.

In addition, a doula will sometimes meet the childbirth educators in her community and, if agreeable with them, attend some classes or review the material they present. What the doula discusses prenatally with parents who attend childbirth education classes will then complement what has been covered in those classes. A doula's instructions, however, will be individualized to the needs of the parents. The support she offers a sixteen-year-old expectant mother, for example, may start at a more basic level and require extra visits.

We believe that in most cases the doula should be engaged separately by the family and not considered a staff member of a hospital. This frees the doula to focus all her attention on the needs of the family. For families without funds, hospitals ideally could offer a list of experienced volunteer doulas or organizations that provide doulas. In certain hospitals the doula is formally part of the program. In any case, the doula has to maintain a delicate balance between respecting the protocol of the hospital and professional staff and at the same time keeping the autonomy of the parents uppermost in her mind. In that way she encourages the parents to advocate on their own behalf, especially during the prenatal period.

An experienced doula becomes respected as an individual who can hear the mother's needs and wishes and, when necessary, interpret them to the medical personnel. For example, if the mother is experiencing much discomfort but wants to continue at her own pace, and the medical personnel believe that a drug for pain relief might be help-

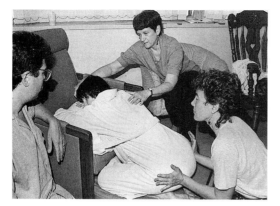

*The father rests within his partner's gaze
as the midwife and doula give support
and helpful counterpressure.*

ful, the doula may help the mother voice her wishes, without becoming confrontative or interfering with the medical staff.

THE DOULA, THE FATHER, AND OTHER FAMILY MEMBERS

A doula often interacts with the expectant mother and with members of the mother's family. She needs to relate tactfully and sensitively to them, not invading their position and sometimes being an adjunct to them. But she also helps the mother express to her family needs that may differ from their expectations or their ways of helping or interacting with her. The doula must tactfully move away from the mother when a close family member such as the hus-band or the laboring woman's own mother arrives to take over the support. The doula then remains nearby, unobtrusive yet ready to provide information. By her words and actions the doula models behaviors and attitudes, that are almost always copied and appreciated by the father. At times a doula needs to be resolutely strong and firm, and at other periods in the labor, tender, soft, and loving.

Throughout the labor and delivery the doula monitors the father's changing relationship to the mother, noting his attitude, skill, and knowledge about labor, his own comfort in touching, and his desire to be useful. (See Chapter 5.) If he is being a good enough support person at meeting most of the mother's needs, the doula can prepare him for what is coming, give suggestions, provide encouragement when he needs support, or spell him when he is exhausted.

A doula has many opportunities to model supportive behaviors for the father. The doula may increase the effectiveness of his support by suggesting that he hold the woman's feet or press a certain area in her back. This gives him something concrete and supportive to do while not overwhelming him with unfamiliar techniques. The doula is sensitive to the fact that even though the mother and father have a good relationship, his touch at certain times may feel like an intrusion to the woman. One doula, having intuitively assessed where a mother felt strong pain and pressure, asked a father to place his hands on his wife and press in that area. The mother, with eyes closed, exclaimed, "That feels wrong." The father, withdrawing his hands, said, "Oh, I'm sorry." The mother replied, "Oh, I didn't mean to hurt you." The doula then had the task of repairing the father's loss of face, his feelings of rejection, and his wife's distress at having hurt him. The doula responded: "It takes time to learn exactly how much pressure to place there. Why don't you hold Sally's feet. It feels good to have someone to press against."

MOTHERING THE MOTHER

After training and experience, a doula often feels an intuitive sense of when to "mother" the mother. This is a vulnerable time when a woman is unusually dependent and open, as she prepares to move through the major maturational change associated with experiencing labor and delivery and with becoming a parent. However, while dependent, a mother still needs the freedom to turn into herself—to take charge at an instinctual level in response to what her body wants to do. It is a paradox, really. A woman in labor needs total support—in order to let go completely, to allow her own system to adapt and respond to the power of the birthing process. This mixed need can be confusing to the mother herself and may be difficult for others to appreciate. Often caregivers find it hard to understand this complex balance: the mother's need to be dependent and independent at the same time.

In certain situations a doula's emotional support may have a deeper therapeutic effect. During birth there is a psychological regression to a woman's own birth, to her essential vulnerability. If a woman has had inadequate or inappropriate mothering herself, the nurturing provided by a doula during this unique period may furnish an opportunity to remother the mother as a person and bring a type of healing to that earlier experience.

To have this effect, a doula needs special skills and insights. A successful doula is comfortable with giving of herself and is not afraid to love. She also can enter another's space and be highly responsive and aware of another's needs, moods, changes, and unspoken feelings. At the same time, she is able to be flexible in this process, adapting herself to each mother's needs, and has no need to control or smother.

The doulas who have been most effective have been secure and confident women who touch easily, hold comfortably, and respond warmly and caringly, but at the same time acknowledge the mother's autonomy. Before she can help a woman in labor, a doula has to be comfortable with birth and not frightened by all the sights and sounds and emotional events that occur during labor and delivery—blood, sweat, screaming, defecation, vomiting, and sometimes crying. A doula must have strength and stamina because the labors are sometimes long and rigorous and may last all night. A doula must be able to remain supportive for the mother who is in pain, even if at times the doula is unable to relieve the discomfort completely. Although her efforts may not appear to be having the desired effect, she must not attempt to deny the pain or the woman's perception of her own experience.

To achieve calm and confidence, a doula needs a comprehensive knowledge of the normal birth process. (See Appendix A in regard to training.) She should be aware of the common situations and delays that occur during labor and recognize those that can be reduced or managed by simple nonmedical interventions, such as changing body position. Training of the doula will prepare her to understand situations that may require medical intervention so she can remain supportive to parents undergoing a difficult labor and birth, or when complications develop. She remains a link to "normalcy," helping the mother retain a sense of accomplishment and self-worth even if the birth does not go as planned.

A doula's presence can be equally valuable for a woman whether she is having her first or a subsequent baby. Mothers having second and third deliveries frequently and enthusiastically express their appreciation for the doula's

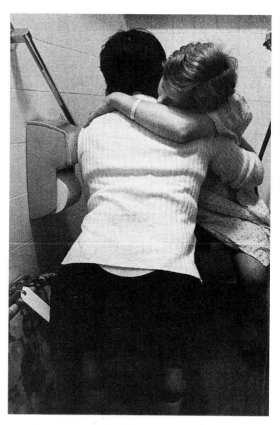

Many women find sitting on a toilet a most helpful position for labor.

emotional support. Those who did not have a doula during their first labor and delivery often say how much they wish they could redo that experience with the help of a doula. And most of those who have had a doula at the birth of their first infant insist they cannot go through another birth without that support. The special bond that develops between the mother and doula during the intense emotional and physical stress of labor and delivery creates a unique relationship. During this experience the woman may be able to move into a deep, safe, securely nurturing enfoldment without losing any part of her autonomy. The doula's support allows the mother's most powerful creativity to emerge in the safest way. This experience often overflows into other respects of a woman's life, enhancing the transformation that childbirth brings about.

As a doula gains experience, she learns how to assess a laboring woman more accurately and gauge both where the woman is in the course of her labor and just what degree of support to give this woman at this stage of labor. For example, some mothers are so tuned in to their own bodies and trust their own systems so much that they are able to go about their labor in an internalized, self-directed manner. Just having the doula in the room is enough support for them.

Other women may seek the comfort and feelings of safety and nurturance that come from a doula who stays very close, holds, caresses, murmurs encouragement, and initiates a variety of measures that enhance a feeling of comfort and security. At the right time the doula will sense a need and move in to hold a hand, caress a shoulder, massage the back, hold an arm or a leg, or support the woman's whole body through a contraction.

At the beginning of labor some women are very uncomfortable with touch by a stranger. The doula must recognize the mother's level of comfort and remain at whatever seems a respectable and comfortable distance. At that stage the doula's communication with the mother will be mainly verbal. As labor progresses most women eventually feel open to touch and then seek, welcome, and respond to more physical contact.

Regarding touch, if a doula is always present as a standard part of a birth program or protocol of the hospital, then even women who are less comfortable with touch are implicitly given permission to ask for it or accept it if they choose. Some women do prefer to labor "alone," in the sense of wanting to be in a quiet, dark, small, protected, and private space. In most hospitals the only such space may be the hospital-room bathroom, but all women want to know that some caring and knowledgeable

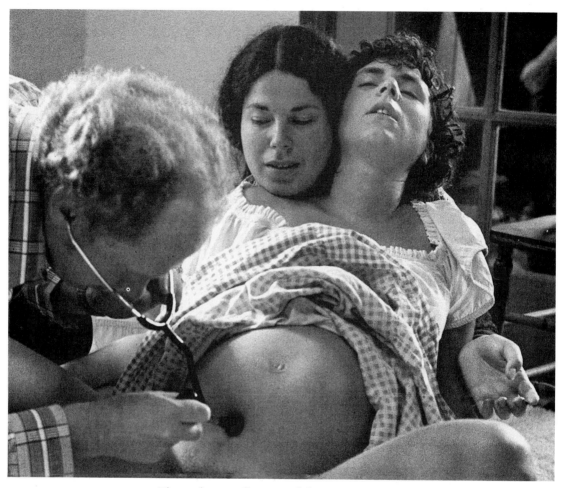

The mother is well-supported during a contraction.

woman is nearby—even if just outside the bathroom door—and ready to help.

Other women want to be held and comforted but are hesitant to ask for that intimacy. The laboring woman often relaxes noticeably when a doula calmly and rhythmically says—while touching the mother's hand or arm—"I am here. I am going to stay with you until the baby is born. I am not going to leave you. We'll see this through together." The fear of the unknown is lessened and relieved. The doula's touch gives an added message of strength to her words.

A number of doulas have noticed that if they are holding a mother's arm while the woman has drifted off to sleep, and then lift their hand off the woman, she immediately awakens, saying, "Don't go"; sometimes, without opening her eyes, she grabs for the doula's hand. The power of touch creates a palpable and comforting enclosure as the doula "mothers" the laboring woman. This reminds us of the literal and figurative holding environment that new mothers create for their infants. The doula's nurturing may somehow be internalized by parents and become a model as they care for their own infant.

Other women look to the doula to take the lead, at times wanting her suggestions and help for position changes, for relaxation, or for reminders to keep their throats open and breathe freely. Many women believe they can labor only when lying on their backs or sides, because they may not know about or appreciate the recent research studies showing shorter and often less painful labor when the woman is walking, especially when the cervix is dilated less than eight centimeters. Also, a hands-and-knees position with the head down helps many women find relief when their cervical dilatation is at ten centimeters. While a woman is laboring in such a position or is walking, the doula and the father give physical support as needed. For example, they may hold the woman's hand while she is walking comfortably and then support her firmly, holding her during a contraction. They may also guide the woman with relaxation breathing throughout the contractions.

Doulas also support women who wish to use visualization and relaxation techniques. Some women may practice imaging with a visualization of the cervix opening, relaxing the muscles in the body, breathing freely, opening the throat, releasing sound and tension, and "letting go." Other women choose imagery that distracts them, focusing for instance on a favorite calm place such as the ocean beach. Still others find it helpful to change a negative image of a contraction to a positive one: that is, if the contraction feels like "a hard rock," they visualize the rock crumbling or turning into sand; or if it feels like an intense build-up of pressure, the mother can try changing the image to a powerful wave that is building up—and then breaking free on the shore. For many of the women who have practiced these techniques, this combination of mental, physical, and behavioral maneuvers appears to create a physiological change in the body that paves the way for the muscles to relax and open.

The experienced doula develops a special sensitivity to and an awareness of the different needs and processes—sometimes very clear, sometimes rather subtle—in the women they serve. Often doulas can reliably predict the stage of cervical dilatation or descent of the baby's head as confirmed by direct examination by the midwife or the physician.

In some cases the woman has greater needs, as with teenagers or women who have been neglected, abused, or mismothered as infants or children. In such cases the doula assumes an extended support role; she will ideally start her work early in pregnancy and continue contact with the mother for as long as a year and a half after the birth of the infant. Some women may have had traumatic or sexually abusive experiences, and birthing may consciously or unconsciously retrigger feelings that stem from these experiences. Doulas learn to work with the mother on language, expressions, and actions that do not restimulate these memories.

When she returns to visit the parents during the postpartum period, the doula is often greeted like an old and dear friend. Often parents bring the baby back to show to the doula six months or a year later. The doulas find it quite natural for the person to whom they have been so close to show pride and affection.

In summary, the doula starts out developing a trusting relationship. Soon she becomes a quiet and calming presence. As labor progresses, she moves to a more intense, stronger nurturing role—pacing herself according to the mother's needs and the power of the birth process itself. Her own role with each mother has this developmental aspect and ends with a close tie, for she has shared one of the great moments in a woman's, and a family's, life.

3

. . .

THE BENEFITS OF DOULA SUPPORT

. . .

Labor support is centuries old, but its advantages have now been validated in six controlled studies and its positive benefits should not be overlooked. . . . The challenge is to turn to obstetric technology only when necessary, relying instead on the practice of continuous labor support to help the birth process follow its natural, normal course.

JOHN KENNELL, MARSHALL KLAUS, ET AL.
Journal of the American Medical Association[17]

· · · IN EVALUATING THE BENEFITS of any particular medical procedure it is important to know whether there is a statistically significant benefit or whether the results could have occurred by chance. Studies of the effects of doula support have been analyzed by precise statistical methods; separately published in the *New England Journal of Medicine*,[36] the *British Medical Journal*,[19] the *British Journal of Obstetrics and Gynaecology*,[12] and the *Journal of the American Medical Association*;[17] and subjected to the usual process of rigorous scientific review.

The crucial evidence that supports the use of doulas comes from six randomized, controlled studies: two in Guatemala, one with 136 women participating and another with 465 women; a study in Houston, Texas, with 416 women participating; and one with 192 women from Johannesburg, South Africa. The fifth and sixth studies done in Helsinki, Finland,[8] and in Canada[11] respectively, although smaller, have also provided support for the use of doulas. In all studies the participating women were expecting their first baby, were healthy, and had had an uneventful pregnancy. Mothers in each of the studies were invited to participate when they arrived at the hospital and were told they might or might not have a woman (the doula) who would stay with them continuously during their labor and delivery, but that they would all receive the same hospital care whether they participated or not.

LENGTH OF LABOR

A woman's first labor is on average much longer than all her subsequent labors. Women approaching their first delivery often worry about the prospects of a long labor. From a medical point of view, the length of a first labor is nature's way of gradually, and carefully dilating the birth passage. As the labor progresses, first the cervix and then the birth canal open and the baby passes through.

The results of the two studies in Guatemala throw a new light on the length of labor for the birth of a first baby. The studies were carried out in an extremely busy obstetric facility. Almost all the women come to the maternity unit of this hospital in early labor when uterine contractions have started but the dilatation of the cervix is only one to two centimeters.

If the mother agreed to participate in the study, she was then assigned at random either to the no-doula or the doula group. The doula learned of her assignment by opening a sealed envelope prepared before the study began. From that moment on, the doulas began to work with the mothers in the doula group, while the no-doula mothers received the usual care. Mothers remained on the ob-

servation ward until the cervical dilatation was three to four centimeters. At that time they were transferred to labor rooms adjoining the delivery rooms. In these Guatemalan studies, hospital policies did not permit any family member or friend to be present in the labor rooms, apparently due to the large number of deliveries (an average of sixty per day) and the limitation of space. There were not enough nurses or aides for one nurse or aide to stay with one particular woman or even in one labor room with six or seven women. The no-doula mothers were thus "alone" for long periods of time during labor.

The exclusion of friends and family reflected the practices on maternity units in the United States twenty to thirty years earlier. It is surprising to reflect that as recently as the 1950s mothers in the United States were laboring alone, usually in a sedated, semiconscious, amnesic state called twilight sleep, with the only support provided by a nurse who usually had responsibility for a number of laboring women. Almost universally, fathers were not allowed to be with their partners during labor and definitely were not allowed in the delivery room. It was this model, but without the twilight sleep, that was transplanted to Guatemalan hospitals by leading U.S. authorities in nursing and medicine. These routines and restrictions had remained frozen in time and were still evident when our studies were done in Guatemala City. (This was in striking contrast to the centuries-old customs of the Mayan Indians living only a few miles away. There a mother was supported by her mother, her mother-in-law, and a native midwife during labor and delivery in her home, and by her mother and mother-in-law in the first postpartum weeks.)

To simplify the evaluation of these studies, we have indicated with each of the following tables whether the results were

not statistically significant   no asterisk
statistically significant   *
highly significant   **

In the first study in Guatemala,[36] the average, or mean, labor length for women in the no-doula group who had routine care (that is, who did not receive oxytocin or have a cesarean section) was nineteen hours, in contrast to the women in the doula group whose labor was only nine hours. The only difference in obstetric care between the two groups of women was the continuous support provided for the doula group.

In our second study the group of mothers in the no-doula group who received routine care again had a longer *average* labor length—15.5 hours, compared to 7.7 hours. As in the first study, the continuous presence of the doula was the only difference in care procedures. There were no significant differences in the age of the mothers, their income, or their living arrangements. However, there was a slightly greater cervical dilatation at admission in the doula group (an average of 1.9 centimeters versus 1.5 centimeters in the no-doula group). When analyzed statistically, a part of the difference in labor length could be explained by the difference in cervical dilatation, but the principal effect was due to the presence of the doula.

2ND GUATEMALAN STUDY

225 women in study (mothers given oxytocin or having cesarean section not included in this analysis of length of labor)

	NO DOULA	DOULA
Length of labor	15.5 hours	7.7 hours**

***Highly significant difference*

1ST GUATEMALAN STUDY

40 women in study (mothers given oxytocin or having cesarean section not included in this analysis of length of labor)

	NO DOULA	DOULA
Length of labor	19 hours	9 hours**

***Highly significant difference*

The third study was carried out in Jefferson Davis Hospital, a large public hospital in Houston, Texas. The number of deliveries in that hospital, which has one of the largest maternity services in the United States, was similar to the number delivered in the Social Security Hospital in Guatemala (15,000 to 17,000 per year). We chose the hospital in Houston because it was a public hospital, and the care of patients by the resident physicians would not vary from mother to mother. That is, there would not be a different approach used by every obstetrician, as is sometimes the case with private obstetricians. Residents in this hospital were required to follow a uniform philosophy and care plan and to use the same indications in all cases for cesarean sections, pain medication, and drugs to stimulate labor.

In some respects the study was a repeat of the two studies[36, 19] in Guatemala. For comparison, it was necessary to examine the benefits, if any, of the doula in a U.S. hospital using modern obstetric methods. In this study, as with the two previous studies, first-time mothers were told about the study, and if they agreed to participate, they were placed by random assignment (sealed envelope) either in a group that would receive support from a doula or in a no-doula group that would have routine care. In this hospital a family member or friend might visit the laboring woman briefly if the labor room was not very busy.

The obstetrical care in this U.S. hospital differed from that in Guatemala in many ways. The study (1984–1987) was

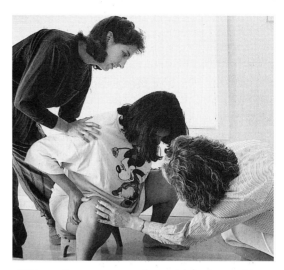

This mother squats on a low stool during pushing, and the doula gives support from behind.

carried out a few years after the Guatemalan studies (1978–1982), and the differences reflected the rapid national and international dissemination of information about new obstetrical procedures and the subsequent changes in care. As was the case in most U.S. hospitals at that time, patients were confined to bed, and an electronic fetal monitor was placed on the abdomen of each mother as soon as she was admitted. Later on in labor, at five centimeters cervical dilatation, the mother's membranes were artificially ruptured so that the monitor could be attached to the baby's scalp, which gave a more direct connection to the fetus. In some situations a catheter was placed in the uterus to measure the strength and regularity of the uterine contractions. Oxytocin, a drug that stimulates uterine contractions, was used frequently to enhance the strength of the contractions. The obstetric staff expected mothers to follow a defined pattern or schedule for the dilatation of the cervix (roughly one centimeter an hour). If the labor did not progress according to this schedule, the obstetricians used measures such as intravenous oxytocin to speed up the labor.

When we began our study, the space limitations in this hospital made it necessary for the staff to require healthy women without complications to be in strong, active labor and to have a cervical dilatation of four centimeters or more before admission to the hospital. Given pressures to restrain hospital costs, most hospitals now have similar policies.

The average length of labor for the group of 212 women supported by a doula was 7.4 hours, in contrast to 9.4 hours for the 204 women in the no-doula group. The difference is highly significant, using statistical tests. The shorter labors in Houston compared to Guatemala were probably related not only to greater cervical dilatation and more advanced stages of labor on admission but also to the fact that the many women given oxytocin were included.

HOUSTON STUDY

416 women (mothers given oxytocin or having cesarean section are included in this analysis)

	NO DOULA	DOULA
Length of labor	9.4 hours	7.4 hours**

***Highly significant difference*

In spite of all the modern obstetrical methods to speed up labor—which include the artificial rupture of membranes, augmentation of the strength of the contractions with oxytocin, and the use of forceps or delivery by cesarean section—the mothers with the shortest labor in our study were again those women who had a doula present throughout their labor.

NATURAL VAGINAL DELIVERIES

In the no-doula group a small number of women (only 25 out of the total 204 in that group, or 12 percent) delivered naturally (that is, vaginally without anesthesia, oxytocin, medication, or forceps), whereas in the doula group the number of women delivering naturally was a surprisingly large 116 out of 212, or 55 percent. It is fascinating to reflect that the presence of one caring woman throughout labor resulted in such a large difference.

HOUSTON STUDY

	NO DOULA	DOULA
No. of mothers with natural vaginal deliveries	25	116**
Total mothers	204	212

**Highly significant difference

USE OF PAIN MEDICATION AND EPIDURAL ANESTHESIA

When the two studies were carried out in Guatemala, there were no anesthesiologists prepared to administer epidural anesthesia for obstetric patients. (This was the case up to 1982 in the majority of hospitals in the United States.) When a forceps delivery or cesarean section was necessary, a general anesthetic was used. In our second study in Guatemala, 1 percent of the women in the doula group were given a narcotic pain medication such as Demerol, in contrast to 4 percent in the no-doula group. Because of the small numbers of women in the study, we could not conclude from this study that the doula was having a significant effect. However, the effects of the doula in Houston in this regard are very interesting. Fifty-five percent, or *more than half*, of the mothers in the no-doula group requested or required epidural anesthesia, which was routinely offered to all mothers when they were admitted to the hospital and when there was evidence of pain. In the doula group only 8 percent of the mothers asked for or required an epidural. (We discuss epidural anesthesia later in this chapter.)

HOUSTON STUDY

416 women

	NO DOULA	DOULA
Mothers receiving epidurals	55%	8%**

**Highly significant difference

Oxytocin provides valuable assistance to some mothers during labor. However, it causes contractions to become more forceful and painful so that mothers managing labor well without any medication often find they need an epidural or other pain medication after oxytocin is started.

In the first Guatemalan study the use of oxytocin was 2 percent in the doula group, compared to 16 percent in the no-doula group. Because the number of women in the study was small, this was not a large enough difference to show statistically whether a doula decreased the need for oxytocin, primarily because it was used so infrequently at that time.

In the second study, 2 percent of the doula-group women needed oxytocin, in contrast to 13 percent in the no-doula group. Since a larger number of mothers were enrolled in this study, this was a meaningful difference, statistically and clinically.

2ND GUATEMALAN STUDY
225 women with uncomplicated labor and delivery requiring no intervention

	NO DOULA	DOULA
Mothers using oxytocin	13%	2%**

**Highly significant difference

In the study in the United States, the percentages were also different. Forty-four percent of the women in the no-doula group were given oxytocin to increase their labor contractions, while only 17 percent of those in the doula group required this medication.

HOUSTON STUDY
416 women

	NO DOULA	DOULA
Mothers using oxytocin	44%	17%**

**Highly significant difference

USE OF FORCEPS

Forceps are special instruments that were developed to provide a safe way to ease the passage of the infant's head through the birth canal. In the past a few babies were injured with the use of forceps when their heads were still high in the birth canal. Most of these unfortunate outcomes were the result of deliveries by physicians whose training and experience were insufficient to develop the skills and judgment needed to use forceps appropriately.

Our experience in an obstetric center where spinal, caudal, or epidural anesthesia has been used over a span of four decades has enabled us to appreciate that the use of low, or "outlet," forceps is often helpful, particularly when epidural, spinal, or caudal anesthesia has been used. When low forceps have been applied by well-trained, experienced obstetricians, there is no harm to the baby. At present, forceps are used in most hospitals and medical centers, but much less often than one or two decades ago.

In Houston 8 percent of the mothers in the doula group had forceps deliveries, which was significantly less than the 26 percent in the no-doula group. These were all low-forceps deliveries. The higher incidence of forceps deliveries in the no-doula group was due in part to the more frequent use of epidural anesthesia. If the simple intervention of support by a doula can reduce the use of forceps to this extent, we must look favorably upon the influence of a doula, whether or not we consider delivery by forceps safe. (In the Guatemalan studies, the number of deliveries in which forceps were used was too small for us to form any conclusions.)

HOUSTON STUDY

416 women

	NO DOULA	DOULA
Forceps deliveries	26%	8%**

*Highly significant difference

NUMBER OF CESAREAN SECTIONS

Statistics collected over many years show it is safer for a healthy mother to deliver her full-term baby vaginally than by cesarean section. Both the mother and the baby face a lower risk of serious complications with vaginal delivery. However, there are some clearly defined reasons for a surgical delivery, such as disproportion between the baby's head and the pelvic outlet.

For several decades in the mid-1900s one measure of a good obstetrical service was that the number of cesarean sections not exceed 5 percent of the total deliveries. However, after close scrutiny of outcomes when babies were in a persistent breech (feet-down) position, physicians proposed that delivering such babies by cesarean section was reasonable. In light of that conclusion and some other ones regarding high-risk and preterm deliveries, physicians anticipated that the incidence of cesarean sections might settle at about 8 to 9 percent. However, the incidence of cesarean deliveries has skyrocketed to levels of 25 to 35 per-

cent, with a few hospitals well above this. This high rate has become a matter of great concern to physicians, women of childbearing age and their families, health insurers, and all those concerned with the physical, emotional, and financial costs.

As a comparison, the National Maternity Hospital in Dublin, Ireland, where every mother has a particular caring midwife with her throughout labor, has had a cesarean-section rate of 5 to 6 percent for the last twenty years. During this period the hospital has had a very low complication rate for mothers and babies. (See Chapter 7.)

Study after study has shown that women who deliver in public hospitals have a lower incidence of cesarean section—without more complications—than those who deliver in private hospitals. As a matter of fact, hospitals that provide care for private patients generally have the highest incidence of cesarean sections, without notable improvement in overall outcome.[4]

In our first study in Guatemala, 19 percent of the women in the doula group needed a cesarean section, in contrast to 27 percent of mothers in the no-doula group. The number of mothers in this study was too small to tell us whether this difference was significant.

In our second study in Guatemala, with a larger number of mothers enrolled, the mothers in the doula group had a 7 percent incidence of cesarean deliveries, in contrast to the 17 percent incidence for mothers in the no-doula group.

2ND GUATEMALAN STUDY
225 women

	NO DOULA	DOULA
Cesarean deliveries	17%	7%*

Significant difference

Hospitals in university medical centers such as the institution where we carried out our study in Houston often have a lower incidence of cesarean deliveries. In spite of this, in the Houston study the mothers in the doula group had a cesarean-section rate of only 8 percent, versus 18 percent in the no-doula group—a significant difference.

HOUSTON STUDY
416 women

	NO DOULA	DOULA
Cesarean deliveries	18%	8%*

Significant difference

In Dublin, Guatemala City, and Houston, when continuous labor support during labor is an integral part of care, the cesarean section rates are remarkably similar: 6 percent, 7 percent, and 8 percent, respectively.

Aside from clear medical indications for cesarean section, some mothers choose a cesarean delivery for what they consider to be a pain-free delivery experience. A number of other women are extremely disappointed that they needed a cesarean, feeling that they have failed to deliver a baby the way nature intended and the way a majority of women manage this important life event. The postoperative discomfort and fatigue when the mother is attempting to meet the urgent demands of the new baby for care and attention have often led to depressed reactions in these mothers in the first weeks after delivery. The recovery time of a mother who has had a cesarean delivery is usually a matter of weeks, in contrast to days after a vaginal delivery.

EFFECTS ON THE MOTHER
AFTER THE DELIVERY

As mentioned, a fourth study of 189 women having their first babies was recently completed by Professor G. Justus Hofmeyer and colleagues of the University of Witwatersand in Johannesburg, South Africa.[12, 41] The doulas in this study were untrained laywomen, who were asked to remain with the laboring women constantly and use touch and verbal communication focusing on three primary factors: comfort, reassurance, and praise. In this study, mothers in the doula group had a significantly lower blood pressure one hour after entry into the study and waited significantly longer before requiring analgesia. However, the other obstetrical outcomes did not show statistically significant differences. This may have been because the mothers who had a doula started the study when further along in their labor. Also, in our research experience the sample size of this study was not large enough to show a significant difference in cesarean-section rates and some other outcomes.

In regard to the effects of doula support during labor on the mother's behavior and attitude after delivery, a hint

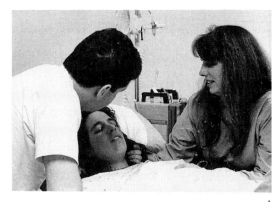

b

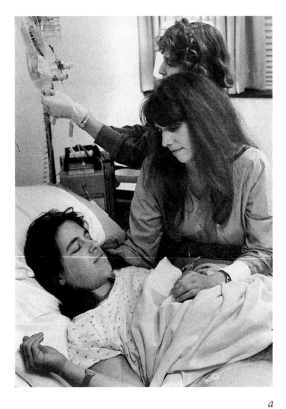

a

(a) Resting early in labor, (b) between contractions late in labor, and (c) the birth.

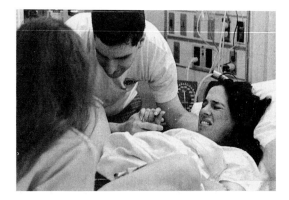

c

of some of the effects found in the Johannesburg study were noted in our first study in Guatemala. Through a one-way mirror we observed both groups of Guatemalan mothers with their babies in the first twenty-five minutes after leaving the delivery room and in a standardized situation. The doula mothers showed more affectionate interaction with their infants, with more smiling, talking, and stroking than the mothers who did not have a doula.

In the Johannesburg study the results showed remarkably favorable effects of constant support during labor on the subsequent psychological health of the women and infants in the doula group in the following areas.

MOTHERS' REPORTS OF PAIN AT 24 HOURS

The one-day postpartum interview results indicated that the doula-group mothers reported less pain during labor and at twenty-four hours after labor. The two groups of mothers had similar levels of anxiety before labor, but the doula group had less at twenty-four hours. Fewer doula-supported mothers considered the labor and delivery to have been difficult, fewer thought it was much worse than they had imagined, and more believed they had coped well during this experience.

BEHAVIOR WITH THE INFANT BY MOTHER'S REPORT AT 24 HOURS

When the mothers were asked about their experiences with their babies, the doula-group mothers spent less time away from their infants. These results suggest that doula support during labor has effects similar to those of mother—infant contact directly after delivery; both appear to increase the mother's interest in her baby and her interaction with the newborn.

MOTHERS' REPORTS ON FEEDING BEHAVIOR AND INFANTS' HEALTH AT SIX WEEKS

Reports given by the mothers in the doula and no-doula groups six weeks after delivery showed a significantly greater incidence of breast-feeding and of feeding the infant on demand in the supported group, and of giving food other than milk in the control group. They indicate a striking difference in the mothers' attitudes and behavior toward their babies. For nurses, pediatricians, and others who care for the health and feeding of children it is most impressive to see a marked difference in the reported incidence of feeding problems: 16 percent in the doula group, versus 63 percent in the no-doula group. What a difference this could mean to parents in terms of worries and doctors bills!

JOHANNESBURG STUDY

Feeding Behavior at Six Weeks	NO DOULA	DOULA
Breast-feeding only	29%	51%**
Demand feeding	47%	81%**
Feeding food other than milk	53%	18%**
Feeding problems	63%	16%**
Average number of days of breast-feeding only	24 days	32 days**

Note: Modified from Wolman[41]
***All highly significant differences*

The information given by the mothers in the doula and no-doula groups about the health of their infants six weeks after delivery was as follows:

Infant Health Problems at Six Weeks	NO DOULA	DOULA
Vomiting	28%	4%**
Colds or runny nose	69%	39%**
Cough	64%	39%**
Poor appetite	25%	0%**

***Highly significant differences*

Diarrhea	33%	19%*

**Significant difference*
Note: Modified from Wolman[41]

These results are striking. There were no differences in hospital admissions and no reasons to expect such differences in the babies, who were similar in all respects at birth. Can the presence of a doula during labor reduce a mother's anxiety sufficiently and give her such a boost in self-esteem that she considers her baby healthier? Or does the mother without a doula perhaps develop a more negative and depressed view of herself and her baby that leads her to look at her infant as more sickly? Certainly a portion of these differences could be related to the increased incidence in the doula group of breast-feeding, which is known to decrease gastrointestinal and respiratory infections.

When the mothers were asked about the amount of time they were away from their baby in a week and the number of days required to develop a relationship, there were again significant differences between the two groups. Mothers in the doula group said they spent 1.7 hours a week away from their baby, in contrast to the no-doula mothers, who were away 6.6 hours. The doula-group mothers said it took them an average of 2.9 days to develop a relationship with their baby, compared to 9.8 days for the other group of mothers.[41]

These results suggest that support during labor expedited the doula-group mothers' readiness to fall in love with their babies and that this attachment made them less willing to be away from their babies. These findings fit with the observations of mother–infant interaction after mothers left the delivery room in the first Guatemalan study.

EMOTIONAL STATE OF MOTHERS

There were impressive differences in the average scores on psychological tests of the mothers in the two groups. On these measures the doula-group mothers showed significantly less anxiety, fewer signs of depression, and a higher level of self-esteem. Although these measures are not sufficient for diagnosing depression, the possibility is suggested by these results. Postpartum depression harms the mother and those who live with her—particularly the infant. If fewer mothers develop this state when supported by a doula there will be great benefits for the mothers themselves, their babies, and their other family members. Mothers who feel better about themselves and are less anxious create a more positive environment for their infants to grow and flourish.

The no-doula-group mothers were more likely to seek medical advice or treatment, a finding consistent with the measure of their emotional state—more anxiety, more depression, and lower self-esteem. Also, they were less likely to bring their babies with them for the six-week postnatal clinic visit. This fits with the doula-supported mothers' reports that they spent significantly more time with their infants than did the no-doula mothers. The doula-supported group of mothers almost always picked up their crying babies, while the no-doula group sometimes picked up their babies and sometimes let them cry. However, more of the doula-supported mothers in this South African study were breast-feeding, and this may account for some of the differences.

RELATIONSHIP WITH PARTNER AT SIX WEEKS

There were no significant differences between the two groups in the womens' satisfaction with their partners before and during the pregnancy. However, some aspect of doula support resulted in doula mothers reporting a great increase in satisfaction with their partner since the birth of the baby and a much greater percentage of mothers who reported their relationship was better right after the birth—more than double the percentage of that in the no-doula group.

Satisfaction with Partner	NO DOULA	DOULA
Before pregnancy	63%	65%
During pregnancy	48%	49%
Since the baby was born	49%	85%**
Relationship better after the birth	30%	71%**

Note: Modified from Wolman[41]
**Highly significant finding

PERCEPTION OF THE BABY AT SIX WEEKS

At six weeks the doula-supported mothers' perceptions of themselves and their babies were clearly more favorable.

Wolman reported that "support group mothers were more positive on all dimensions involving the specialness, ease, attractiveness and cleverness of their babies." A higher percentage of supported mothers not only considered their babies beautiful, clever, and easy to manage but also believed their infants cried less than other babies. In fact, the supported mothers believed that their babies were "better" when compared to a "standard baby"; whereas the no-doula mothers perceived their babies as "just slightly less good as" or "not as good as" a "standard baby." Wolman said that "support group mothers also perceived themselves as closer to their babies, as managing better, and as communicating better with their babies than control group mothers did." A higher percentage of the doula-supported mothers reported that they were pleased to have their babies, found becoming a mother was easy, and felt that they could look after their babies better than anyone else could. In contrast, the no-doula group of mothers perceived their adaptation to motherhood as more difficult and felt that others could care for their baby as well as they could.[41]

Such far-reaching effects for the supported mothers are striking. While the period of labor is a relatively short time in a woman's life, it is also a time of extraordinary stress and need—a crisis in the original sense of the word, that is, a turning point.

MATERNAL FEVER AND EPIDURAL ANESTHESIA

With the high quality of obstetrical and newborn care provided for healthy mothers and infants in a teaching hospital in the United States, we did not expect that there would be a difference in the health of the infants in the two groups. In the Houston hospital, all full-term babies were routinely discharged home before forty-eight hours of age unless a medical problem arose. We were quite surprised to find a difference in the number of babies who had an extended stay in the hospital. Ten percent of the babies in the doula group and 24 percent of the newborn infants in the no-doula group were kept in the hospital. The difference was unrelated to the health of the mother and did not include babies who stayed when the mother had a cesarean delivery.

HOUSTON STUDY

	NO DOULA	DOULA
Infants kept more than 2 days in hospital	24%	10%*

Significant difference

When we looked at the reasons for these babies being held for an excessively long stay, we did not find any actual differences in the health status of the infants in the two groups during their time in the hospital. Then, after examining the course of these babies more closely, we found that the main reason for the differences between the two groups was that more mothers in the no-doula group had developed a fever during labor. This occurred with 10 percent of the mothers in the no-doula group, and 1 percent of the mothers in the doula group.

HOUSTON STUDY

	NO DOULA	DOULA
Maternal fever	10%	1%*

Significant difference

When a mother develops a fever during labor, physicians recognize this as a warning the baby may have a serious and potentially fatal, but uncommon, bloodstream infection called septicemia (sepsis). However, because the risk of not treating a baby with sepsis is great, and because the diagnosis at the time of birth is difficult and existing antibiotics are effective, babies of mothers with fever are usually considered to have sepsis and are treated until the cultures are reported to be negative. Even though babies of mothers with fever may appear normal at birth, they will have cultures of their blood and spinal fluid taken immediately and will usually be started on intravenous or intramuscular antibiotics until their overall condition and the results of the cultures are known, usually within three days. As there is no previous experience with the appearance and behavior of an individual newborn baby, maternal fever may be the only clue to a life-threatening infection. To wait until more clear-cut signs of infection appear is to risk the life of the baby.

When we investigated possible reasons for the fever, we found that the mothers who had a fever were significantly more likely to have had epidural anesthesia. A probable explanation for this high incidence of maternal fever in the no-doula group comes from research in England.[6] This study shows that when a mother has epidural anesthesia during labor, her temperature slowly but steadily rises; if labor is long enough, the temperature will reach the level of a fever. Long labors and epidurals were more common in the no-doula group, so chances were greater that mothers in that group would develop a fever.

It is difficult for physicians to be sure whether an individual mother's fever is due to epidural anesthesia or to sepsis in the baby. In other words, the association of maternal fever with an epidural unfortunately does not help the obstetrician or pediatrician decide whether a specific mother's fever is caused by infection or by the epidural anesthesia. However, the decreased need for pain relief during labor when a doula provides support would lessen the number of epidurals and therefore the number of women who have fevers and the number of babies who have to be evaluated for illness.

EPIDURAL ANESTHESIA RECONSIDERED

In the last decade the percentage of mothers who have had an epidural anesthetic during labor and delivery has escalated. The development and spread of the epidural technique in obstetrics has been of particular benefit for women who require cesarean delivery, because the mother is then awake and aware of what is going on.

In contrast to the agreement on the use of epidurals for cesarean deliveries, there are differing opinions about the effects of epidural anesthesia for healthy women likely to have a normal labor and delivery. Many anesthesiologists describe the epidural as the "Cadillac of anesthesias." They point out its ideal effect of providing control of pain throughout the long period while the cervix is gradually dilating. At times labor that has been progressing slowly may speed up after epidural anesthesia is started. The anesthesiologists further note that epidural anesthesia can be controlled so that the mother has a return of some sensation after full dilatation of the cervix as the baby's head descends through the birth canal. This means that the normal neuromuscular forces that guide and turn the baby's head and the normal involuntary "pushing," or expulsion, reflexes can be intact. For women who believe they cannot tolerate the pain of labor contractions, it is fortunate that epidural anesthesia is available not only to relieve their pain and anxiety about it but also to allow them to be fully awake.

Many of the medical publications discussing the use of epidural analgesia have been positive. In addition, word-of-mouth communication from mother to prospective mother has also been favorable. As a result of these reports and other factors such as the availability of an obstetrical anesthesiologist around the clock in many hospitals, the incidence of obstetrical epidural anesthesia use has soared to 80-plus percent of deliveries in some institutions.

Many experienced nurses, midwives, and obstetricians report, however, that this anesthetic method often does not measure up to the ideal. Labor that has been progressing normally may slow down or stop when an epidural is started. The length of labor may be extend-

Deep in concentration, support from both the father and doula.

ed, as was the case in our Houston study. The pain relief is not always complete, and in spite of the development of continuous methods of administering the anesthetic, its effectiveness may fluctuate. A major disadvantage is that once the epidural is started, the mother is no longer able to walk around or change body positions easily. Also, attempts to start an epidural are sometimes unsuccessful. Frequently, the anticipated tapering off of the anesthetic's effects, which would reestablish muscle tone and the pushing reflex, is not achieved. Therefore, the descent of the baby's head through the birth canal is often slow and more difficult because of the lack of the normal reflex responses in the mother's body that turn the head into the optimal delivery position and push out the baby. This stage of labor consequently is often prolonged, and de-

livery by forceps, vacuum extraction, or cesarean section is often required. In addition, researchers in England, have also discovered a significant increase in backaches among mothers who have had epidural anesthesia. Of the women who reported backache, 69 percent had it for more than a year after giving birth.[26]

Two other studies suggest that there may be important side effects of epidural anesthesia.[14, 15] Neither of these are randomized, controlled trials, so the results cannot be considered conclusive. One was a large retrospective study in Texas[38] that showed an increased cesarean-section rate for mothers who had had epidural analgesia. The other study involved an analysis of the results for women in the Houston study who had had epidural analgesia in the first stage of labor compared to those who had not. (Note, however, that this study was designed to test the effect of the doula, not of epidural analgesia.) Those given epidural analgesia for pain in the first stage of labor had had a significantly higher percentage not only of cesarean and forceps deliveries but also of oxytocin use. More women given epidurals had had a prolonged second stage of labor (the descent of the baby's head down the birth canal to delivery), a diagnosis of failure to progress, and longer labors.

Before mothers and fathers tell their physician or midwife that they insist on an epidural for pain relief, they would do well to pause and reflect on these and other considerations. Although the drug used for an epidural goes into a small space just outside the woman's spinal cord, the medication does get into the mother's bloodstream and then into the baby. Babies therefore have mild to moderate changes in their behavior in the first hours and days. As we said earlier, a woman who has an epidural has a progressive rise in temperature as labor proceeds. This does not occur with natural childbirth or with other pain medication. The mother's rising temperature is associated with an increase in the baby's heart rate, which could incorrectly be interpreted as distress in the baby associated with, for example, an interference with the supply of oxygen. Together with the concern that the baby might have a serious infection, these signs put pressure on the attendants to deliver the baby as soon as possible. This may result in a cesarean or forceps delivery, because the baby's condition may remain unclear until after delivery and close examination.

In addition, as suggested earlier, a number of mothers have told us about their disappointment that they failed to go through labor without medication. They were "unable to do what any uneducated peasant mother could do." The percentage of mothers disturbed by this varies with different populations and ap-

pears to be related to their expectations and their view of the birthing experience. Because they had an epidural, these women express their sadness that they have missed out on the sense of accomplishment that they had expected.

The directors of some obstetrical services have been concerned about these side effects of epidural anesthesia and its influence on mothers' behavior with their babies. However, there is still a lack of unbiased, randomized, controlled clinical trials of epidural analgesia, and there has been relatively little study of the effects of epidural anesthesia on the normal shifts and surges of hormones thought to be associated with unmedicated mothers' intense desire to hold and interact with their infants after delivery. Some experienced obstetricians have concerns that the usual ecstatic enthusiasm of mothers toward their new infants common after an unmedicated delivery has been lost, delayed, or minimized. They comment that the mothers who have had epidural anesthesia do not get the same feeling of accomplishment or boost in self-esteem as those who deliver without an epidural. While anesthesia, including epidurals, has been a godsend in complicated deliveries, a well-conducted, unanesthetized delivery can provide a new mother with special enthusiasm and a great burst of ecstasy for the "birth of her family."

FINANCIAL CONSIDERATIONS

In addition to the psychological and physical benefits of labor support, there are important financial ones. Anesthesia costs could be cut significantly if more doula-supported women labored and delivered without anesthesia or with a local. Expenses could be reduced as fewer infants born to doula-supported women required an extended hospital stay.

By conservative estimates cesarean sections are performed in about 20 to 25 percent of all U.S. births each year. Let us assume, on the basis of the Houston study, that the cesarean rate with a doula could be cut from 20 percent to 10 percent. This decrease and the accompanying shortening of maternal hospital stays and reduction of operating room expenses, need for skilled delivery and postpartum staff, and medication use would mean a savings for individual families of about $3,500. Even when the additional cost of the doulas' services are included, the total medical care costs for the nation could be reduced by more than $2 billion annually.

A reduction in the use of epidural anesthesia to 8 percent from the current 80 to 90 percent in some hospitals could mean savings to the parents of about $1,300 per delivery—a mammoth saving nationwide, given that more than four million births occur each year in the United States.

CONCLUSIONS

Recently, the authors have completed an analysis that draws together the six randomized trials described above with a technique known as a "meta-analysis." When the results of these six studies are calculated together, the presence of a doula reduces the overall cesarean rate by 50 percent, length of labor by 25 percent, oxytocin use by 40 percent, pain medication by 30 percent, the need for forceps by 40 percent, and requests for epidurals by 60 percent.[21]

These convincing research findings about the many benefits of doula care confirm our overall conclusions: doula support enhances the well-being of mothers and babies, leads to fewer medical interventions in the process of labor and delivery, and saves money for individuals and hospitals. The findings provide a strong argument for expansion of doula services.

4

· · ·

BIRTH WITH A DOULA

· · ·

[A mother] is in need of the nurse's [read doula's] presence, and of her power to help in the right way, and at the right moment, should something go wrong. But all the same, she is in the grip of natural forces and of a process that is as automatic as ingestion, digestion and elimination, and the more it can be left to nature to get on with it the better it is for the woman and the baby.

D. W. WINNICOTT
Babies and Their Mothers [40]

· · · TO MAKE CLEAR THE REAL-
life role of a doula, we followed the labor and delivery of a couple expecting
their first baby. Two to three months
before the birth, Lydia and Dan began
to consider engaging a doula. Lydia,
thirty-three, is an administrative assistant in a large company, and Dan, thir-
ty-six, is an electronics engineer. Both
parents were delighted about having a
baby and shared their experience in
detail.

Initially they had a difference of opin-
ion about a doula. Dan was not sure he
saw the benefits of having a third person. "The drawback was in my mind
that a doula would take away from the
intimate experience of having this baby
by ourselves—only us and the baby. It
looked like an interference to me."

Lydia saw the issue differently. She
was concerned about the possibility of
pain. She did not view the birth as an
intimate experience but rather "as being
something that could conceivably be
pretty painful, and you should do everything you possibly could to make it
better."

In the next month Lydia saw Dan's decision change when during a childbirth
class they viewed a film depicting the last
ten minutes of delivery for five or six
mothers. Lydia said afterwards it looked
to both of them like a very intense experience. "I saw his mind wonder that
maybe it might be more helpful to have

somebody there, because it seemed like a pretty difficult thing to do."

Dan began to see the labor as a potentially very painful experience for Lydia and thought that a doula "might make it a bit easier by having more security. She might make the whole experience last a shorter time, and this way you'd experience less pain."

When he learned that the doctor only arrived in the last hour or so, that the nurse would be taking care of two or more patients, and that consequently they would often be left by themselves, they both then agreed that a doula was a good idea.

After interviewing three doulas, they chose Mary Frances, an experienced doula in her early fifties. They felt she was warm, caring, gentle, and friendly. She had a child of her own and had assisted in a large number of births, which made Lydia feel more comfortable.

The doula made arrangements to visit them four times in the two months before the due date to learn about their expectations and to discuss various aspects of labor and delivery with which first-time parents may not be familiar. This allowed them to talk in more detail with their obstetrician. The biggest issue was that Lydia wanted to try to have an unmedicated birth, but if she decided on an epidural during labor, she did not want any argument about it. In these discus-sions Mary Frances recognized that Lydia was "a strong person. I felt pretty confident that she was going to be okay and could make her needs known in either case."

At the first meeting the doula discussed the couple's plans and wishes in general. At the next visit she demonstrated visualization and relaxation techniques. At the third visit she showed Lydia and Dan a series of birth positions that might be useful during labor, followed by a fourth visit when they toured the hospital together. Mary Frances also introduced her backup doula to the couple. Mary Frances taped a progressive relaxation and birth visualization sequence and asked Lydia to listen to it several times. Mary Frances would then use many of these phrases during the actual birth, which would activate many of the suggestions already taken in at an unconscious level.

During one of the visits, Lydia had many questions for the doula about the birth. This was now near the time of labor, and Lydia was feeling especially tired. She wanted to know what types of things the doula would do if she were feeling pain. Dan was interested in the doula's perception of what might happen during the entire birth. Lydia noted that it was very helpful to her to talk to an experienced woman about some of her worries. Lydia, Dan, and the doula gained from these visits, each learning about the other. The doula noted, "I really like these prenatal visits. You get to know the couple, and then you can build up some trust."

The doula made plans to come to Lydia and Dan's home during early labor. Lydia also mentioned that her sister Lynne, to whom she was close, would be coming to the labor. Lydia was concerned, however, about the potential for her sister to become very anxious during times of stress. Lydia told her sister that if she became too anxious during labor, she would have to leave.

Labor began two weeks after their last visit, very nearly on the expected date, at 5:30 A.M., with rupture of the membranes. Dan and Lydia, both excited, called Lynne at 6 a.m., wanting to catch her before she left for the day. She drove over soon afterward.

Lydia took a long shower, which she found relaxing, and then she and Dan had a nice big breakfast, "because I'd heard that you needed to keep your strength up." They timed the contractions, which were getting stronger. They talked to the doula, Mary Frances, at 7:30 A.M., and she said to call the doctor. The doctor told them to come to the hospital when the contractions were three to five minutes apart and a certain length. Within a half hour it was time. They quickly called the doula to meet

them there, since there was not time for her to come to their home. When they arrived at the hospital, the doula was waiting for them.

Dorothy, the nurse, took Lydia's blood pressure, asked her many questions, and checked her cervical dilatation. Lydia noted, "She said I was 100 percent effaced* and three centimeters dilated. I thought we were pretty far along. I knew I had to go to ten centimeters, but I thought three centimeters was a pretty good number to come in with.

"Dorothy the nurse started to ask me questions while I was having a contraction. I remembered from my childbirth class that if somebody's talking while you're having a contraction, the husband should say, 'She's having a contraction. Could you please wait.' He didn't pipe up with that, so I said, 'I'm having a contraction—I'll answer you when I'm finished.'

"She asked me the question again; she had ignored what I'd said, which worried me. She was a knowledgeable person—she did give good suggestions—and sometimes she tried to be nice. But she must have had some kind of chip on her shoulder, because when we first

*Effacement is the thinning out of the cervix, expressed as a percentage of its full thickness. At 100 percent it is completely flattened out.

walked in and she saw my sister Lynne, she said, 'Oh, you have Mary Frances, and you have your sister, too'—as if this other person was an extra burden on her, or was going to be. She couldn't believe we had three people, even though this hospital said it's okay, and my doctor said it's fine. I thought that the hospital should be able to handle it when a couple had more people.

"Dorothy then said, "You may need to have an epidural. It's a first baby; it's going to be a long labor. I want you to see the anesthesiologist.' I mentioned that I'd had an epidural for knee surgery and knew what it was. She said, 'But I want you to have a pleasant experience.' This was a strange thing for me to hear.

"It seemed to me that everything was progressing very rapidly, and I didn't see any point in it. I thought, If we can do it without the epidural, why not? I can tolerate a lot of pain. It's only for one day. It's worth it. The doula, Mary Frances, was in the room, and she was watching and being supportive. Everybody was there."

Mary Frances's recollection of this period adds a similar perspective. "I never got the feeling that the nurse was really with Lydia. When the nurse came in, she had a list of questions and a form to fill out. At one point Lydia started to have a contraction, and she indicated for the nurse to wait. I was watching the nurse, and she just was impatient—'Let's get on with this.' I thought, Oh dear, this isn't looking good.

"I don't see myself as somebody who should intervene, if the communication is something that is working. I need to stay out of it, because otherwise, I'm taking away the mother's power if I get in there.

"The nurse checked her at that point, and she was three centimeters. Then the nurse left. Early on, nurses are mostly out of the room, which is one of the reasons I think that a childbirth assistant is necessary in a hospital." Mary Frances pointed out that many nurses are much more supportive, but that pressures in many hospitals make it hard for them to remain attentive.

From 9:30 A.M. until 11:00 A.M. Lydia reported she was most comfortable when she was walking around the room or sitting in the shower. Dan mainly accompanied her in walking. Lydia said that breathing through the contractions with the doula was the most helpful tool, whether walking or in the shower. When she was lying in bed, she changed sides often and continued the breathing with Mary Frances. "At this time the doula was very useful to me. I felt she was very calm, and I felt I wanted to look at her face and I wanted to breathe with her. Around 11:00 A.M. the doula noticed that my legs were shaking and

The tender affection of the father and the quiet support of the doula.

my skin was flushed. She suggested that I might be much further along in transition."

When the nurse came in to check at 11:00 A.M., Mary Frances vividly remembers what happened next.

"The nurse proceeded to tell her how great she was doing. 'You're really on top of your breathing; you're really doing wonderfully.' And then she paused for a minute and said, 'But you really don't have to experience all this pain if you don't want to.' I thought, What is this?

"And she said, 'You know, you can have an epidural, and it won't have any effect on you or your baby whatsoever.'

"I told an anesthesiologist friend of mine that a nurse had said this, and he was concerned because it's not the facts. I was annoyed because Lydia was feeling a lot of pain and she was on top of it, but it was there. To have this carrot held out to you: that you don't have to feel this pain, and that it's not going to affect you or your baby. Lydia said to the nurse, 'What I'd like to do is have an unmedicated birth.' It was like the nurse didn't hear it. She said, 'I'd like you just to talk with the anesthesiologist,' and left to fetch him."

The doula noted: "It's easier for nurses if the mother has the epidural, and then she's on the monitor, and then they see everything from their station. Not all nurses recommend epidurals like this. I don't think that those who do really understand what they're taking away from the mother.

"Lydia said she'd talk to the anesthesiologist if the nurse wanted her to. But she said again, 'I'd really like to have an unmedicated birth.' I thought, 'God bless her, just to be able to get that out in the face of all this pain and this woman.'

"The nurse came back fifteen minutes later to check Lydia and found that she was in transition at eight centimeters, having made great progress. The anesthesiologist came in but didn't push the epidural. He said to Lydia. 'It's up to you.' He did talk about the possible side effects. He mentioned that the urge to push could be diminished."

The doula remembers offering Lydia support in whatever choice she made. Mary Frances said, "I wanted her to know that she was doing great—that she was really doing well."

The doula noted that Dan and Lynne were both helpful. "Dan never left the room," Lydia remembers. "He had a good expression on his face that made me feel good. It was also helpful when he held my hand or leg. My sister was really helpful when I was pushing and I needed her also to hold my leg."

In the pushing stage, from that time until the birth of the baby, Lydia alternated between two positions: either squatting and supporting herself by holding onto a bar or propping up in bed with Mary Frances at her side helping her breathe, and Dan and Lynne holding her legs so she could push against them. The doctor was now present, checking and encouraging. They remember it as a real team effort.

Lydia described it thus: "During the pushing, Lynne and Dan sort of jumped in and started helping, and I felt they were being more effective. We were trying to figure what was the best way to progress in pushing. They brought a mirror in, and they were so excited. The three of them, especially Dan and Lynne, were so excited. When I finally saw it in the mirror, I thought it was slow. I thought it was going to be faster than that. It was very hard. It was very difficult and painful.

"I felt I was directing them by saying, 'Here it comes again.' Then they would come and lift my legs up. We were sort of chatting in between the contractions. They weren't very far apart. No medicines. I had a little bit of water. Mary Frances was wiping my forehead occasionally.

"I liked my team. They were great. Afterwards I think we all felt like a team—that we did a good job, that everybody had played an important role, a good part. I felt good about Mary Frances.

"Everybody would sort of comment on how good the pushing was: 'Oh, you're doing great. Keep going.' They were always very encouraging, partly, I think, because we had discussed that we wanted to always have encouraging thoughts going on. 'Things are going well. That was a good push'—repeating those things over and over again. 'You can see the head crowning. Look at the hair.' So usually I had a good gauge on how my pushing was going. But at one point, listening to them, I couldn't tell whether I was effective or not.

"I thought, If I got up off this table and started to leave, these people wouldn't let me leave the room. I said to Dan, 'I want to go home.' The doctor at that point said, 'Give me your hand,' She took my hand and put it on top of the baby's head. I could feel her head coming out even thought it wasn't all the way out. The doctor said, 'One of my laws is, If you can touch it, you can push it out.' "

Lydia continued: "The birth of the baby took only another five or eight minutes. At 1:45 P.M. an eight-and-a-half-pound healthy baby girl was born. During this time the doula never left my side. She wiped my forehead. She was the one who noticed how I was feeling. Lynne and Dan were more interested in the baby. The doctor kept leaving and coming back, since she had two other deliveries that day. The doula was more caring about how I looked, if I was hot; she was concerned that things were taken care of for me quickly, whatever I asked for. She took care of me."

The next day the doula came into the

First inspection.

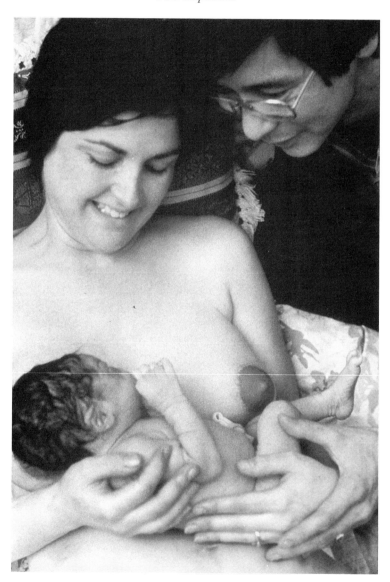

hospital to visit Lydia and Dan. Together they went over how the labor and birth went. Lydia noted: "Mary Frances said I did a good job, I was very strong. I wasn't sure I had done a good job. I didn't feel bad about it, but she confirmed I did a good job. It was really kind of amazing how well it went. I think the doula kept me from having medication. She kept my resolve up. It's hard to say if she speeded up the labor or not, but she certainly made me feel more comfortable."

Dan added at this point: "It was a good experience. I was able to be more relaxed because some of the pressure was off me. We needed the extra person physically to help Lydia and emotionally because the nurse didn't provide that help. The doula's presence was critical to the atmosphere because the nurse was very pessimistic."

5
. . .
A FATHER'S TRUE ROLE
. . .

*I've run a number of marathons. I've done a lot of hiking
with a heavy backpack, and I've worked for forty hours
straight on-call; but going through labor with my wife was
more strenuous and exhausting than any of these experiences.
We could never have done it without the doula.
She was crucial for us.*

A FATHER

· · · FOR FIRST-TIME FATHERS, the labor and delivery unit of a hospital is a strange place with strange smells, sights, and sounds, including the cries of women in labor. Even more stressful are the changes occurring in the mothers, the people they love most—obvious pain, anxiety, unusual sounds, and fluid discharges never seen before. The changes in the appearance of laboring women can be extremely distressing to new fathers, as can the women's sometimes dramatic changes in behavior—becoming alternately overwhelmed, demanding, desperate, and even antagonistic. Fathers also face the dilemma of what to do and where to stand, how much to touch and what kind of touch to offer, and how much loving affection to show in front of strangers. The stress is increased by the fathers' feelings of direct responsibility for the women's distress and the added responsibility, in some cases, of making significant decisions about the medical care during labor.

From the available information and our own experience, we believe that too much is expected of men in childbirth today. Fathers cannot be objective; there is too much at stake. There is anticipation and excitement, mixed with concern and anxiety about the potential danger, and the unknown. No matter how much experience a father may have had with childbirth, he cannot remain emotionally distanced enough to meet both his own and the mother's needs at this intense time. In suggesting the support of a doula, our intent is not to diminish the father's role but to enhance it, to free him up to stand by the mother. With the doula present, the father is never left as the sole, isolated, responsible person caring for the laboring mother. This vital ingredient—the support of an experienced woman—has been lost in modern obstetrical care.

A father needs to be present: a mother needs to know he is there, he is with her, loving, concerned, responsive, and taking responsibility for his new child. His presence is important for the emotional connection of the couple and for their relationship to each other and to the baby. Recognition and validation of the father's right and need to be present at the birth of his infant is not only compatible with but also enhanced by the presence of a doula.

FATHERS AT DELIVERY

Having fathers present during childbirth is a fairly recent practice. When Queen Victoria's husband was present for the birth of the future Edward VII in 1841, the British medical journal, the *Lancet*, printed a lively series of letters about his presence. In her book, *Midwives and Medical Men*, Dr. Jean Donnison noted

that a "Country Doctor" protested the intrusion and condemned the father's presence as a "new upper class fashion."[5] Other physicians, she noted, commented that the father's presence at childbirth was "indecent, unbecoming, unnecessary and contrary to nature." However, some argued at the time that many wives welcomed their husband's presence, support, and help at the birth. Interestingly, a lay writer wondered why it was an indelicate intrusion for the husband to be present but acceptable for the doctor—a man and a stranger.

Although the majority of births in the United States had shifted from home to hospital by the end of the 1930s, it was not until the 1970s that the majority of hospitals began to permit fathers to be present during labor. In 1973 only 27 percent of women delivering in a U.S. hospital were accompanied by the baby's father; by 1983, 79 percent had such accompaniment.

Though fathers have been permitted to come into the labor and delivery suite, they have not always been welcomed openly. Often this shift in hospital policy has been dictated by marketing pressures, to maintain or increase the number of deliveries. This policy change, attributed to the current interest in family-centered maternity care, has often given only lip service to the father's presence. Obstetricians and nurses

The beginning.

display a wide range of comfort levels with fathers during labor—from easy acceptance to grudging toleration of their presence. During any given labor, a father may be greeted warmly and accepted by some caregivers and almost rejected by others. Complicating the father's role as a steady source of emotional support for the mother is the routine practice of some medical personnel to ask the father to leave every time a medical procedure, such as a vaginal examination or the starting of an epidural, takes place—just when the mother may be needing someone the most.

In addition to the varying degrees of acceptance of the father by the obstetrician and hospital staff are variations in the father's own ability to be supportive, as well as in the woman's desire to have him be her main emotional support. Drawing on the strong evidence now available from six separate randomized trials in which doulas have been the supportive companions, we can compare doulas' and fathers' behavior and effectiveness of a support. Do the father and a doula care for the mother in a similar fashion during labor? Is there a difference in their roles, or is there a difference in the type of support a woman in labor needs from a woman and that which she needs from a man? Are the needs of each parent being addressed during labor and delivery? Are fathers being pushed into a situation where they do not feel comfortable? And are they excluded from meaningful moments?

Current views of the ideal role for fathers vary tremendously: from fathers as mere observers to fathers as fill-ins for busy personnel, as "advisors" or as actual decision makers about the birth process. For example, some doctors address the father and ignore the mother when discussing what is happening and making

Early labor, a mother's nervousness, a father's excitement.

decisions about what procedure to do next. In other situations some anxious fathers take the prerogative to go to the nurses' station and ask that a nurse perform a particular procedure, such as providing pain medicine, as soon as possible. Sometimes fathers and medical personnel do not communicate clearly. For example, confusion may arise when the obstetrician tells a father, "I believe we possibly should give an epidural." The father may interpret this statement as a question, while the obstetrician has, in fact, just made a decision to give an epidural. The other side of the continuum is that a small number of caregivers consider all fathers to be in the way. Sadly, some fathers also believe this description.

DOULAS AND FATHERS: TWO DIFFERENT ROLES

To help understand and compare the roles of the doula and father during birth, we have closely observed and recorded their behaviors during early and late labor. The information was gathered in two studies: in one study the behavior of twelve fathers was observed in a Cleveland hospital, and in the other study three doulas were observed caring for thirteen mothers in a Houston hospital. The same techniques and forms were used to record the findings from the two studies.[2] The investigators in both studies assessed and then later compared behaviors during one hour in early labor (less than seven centimeters cervical dilatation) and one hour in late labor (more than seven centimeters dilatation). The behaviors of the fathers and doulas were analyzed only for the periods when the mother was uncomfortable or having a contraction.

Overall, fathers were present for somewhat less time during the labor than were the doulas. In early labor fathers were in the mothers' rooms 78 percent of the time, while in late labor they were in the rooms 95 percent of the time. Both in early and late labor the doulas remained with the mothers almost 100 percent of the time.

Throughout early and late labor the doulas remained closer physically (less than one foot) to the mothers 85 percent of the time, while the fathers were that close for only 28 percent of the time. During actual contractions, the doulas were again closer to the mothers than were the fathers, both in early and late labor. Fathers held the mothers' hands a greater percentage of time than did the doulas in early labor, but this reversed in late labor. Overall, the fathers and the doulas held the mothers' hands about the same length of time. Both fathers and doulas talked much more in late labor than in early labor.

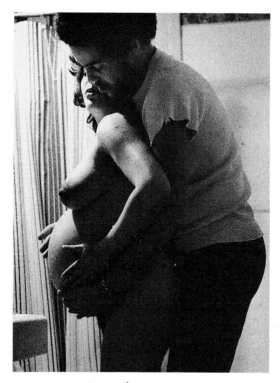

Strong, loving support.

When all forms of touching were tallied, a difference was noted. (Touching here included rubbing, stroking, clutching, and holding.) During both the early and late periods the doulas were touching the mothers more than 95 percent of the observation time, compared to less than 20 percent for the fathers. The fathers watched the fetal monitors much more than did the doulas.

Interestingly, another ongoing study of fathers has noted that their behavior is altered when they are not the only person responsible for support. When a doula supported a couple throughout labor, the father was freed to offer more personal support and did much more intimate touching of the mother's head and face.

The differences between doulas and fathers need some explanation. This was the first time these men had been present with a woman during labor, in contrast to the extensive labor and delivery experience of the doulas. The fathers appeared uncertain about what to do, and they were deferential to the nursing and medical staff, often retreating from the mother when a nurse or physician entered the room. Later in labor when the contractions were more painful, fathers may have retreated because of exhaustion and an intolerable level of concern. A doula with experience and no personal tie to the woman in labor could pace herself and not become anxious about behaviors and events that she knew were part of normal labor. We suspect that in some cases the father's behaviors, like sleeping or leaving late in labor were a consequence of his anxiety that his wife might die.

We actually make demands on first-time fathers that exceed those made on medical students. For many years we have taken groups of first-year medical students who have had some experience in hospitals or emergency rooms into special hospital divisions such as the neonatal intensive care unit, the coronary care unit, or the burn unit. In almost every situation there are two or three medical students who become pale and sweaty and need to leave.

Although the fathers performed differently than the doulas in our two studies, in these and other studies more than 90 percent of the mothers stated, when questioned after delivery about the presence of the father, that it was extremely important that the father had been able to be with them. All of the fathers replied that it was extremely important for them to be present during this experience. In the majority of cases both parents found positive meaning and mutual support in the sharing of childbirth.

On many occasions we have observed the following: The mother in labor was so interested in having the father remain with her throughout the delivery that she was devoting much of her attention and energy to his comfort and well-being. She would often turn to him as he sat in a chair and say, "You must be hungry—why don't you go to the cafeteria and eat a meal? I will be all right while you are away." And then later, "You look tired. You got up very early this morning. Perhaps you should take a nap." We have been impressed with the sensitivity and thoughtfulness of obstetric nurses to this reversal of support roles during labor. Often the nurse, overhearing the mother, would promise to look after the father, and would also emphasize that it was the mother who needed support and that she needed to focus on her needs. The doula supporting the couple always thinks about what will be most helpful for both the mother and the father.

Since we noted in Chapter 3 that the doula's presence has various beneficial effects on the medical outcome of the mother's labor and delivery, we might ask what effect the father has on the birth process. To date, the available studies have compared a woman's birth with or without the baby's father, but without any comparison with a doula. Though the majority of studies show that the presence of the father significantly reduces the pain medications (such as Demerol) required by the mother,[9, 34] no study has yet reported a decrease in the length of labor, the incidence of forceps use, the rate of cesarean sections, the incidence of epidural anesthesia, or the use of oxytocin.

HOW FATHERS EXPERIENCE BIRTH

It is important to remember that each father and mother comes to the delivery with different life histories, and birth evokes within each of them different feelings and responses that are often unexpected not only within themselves but with each other. To illustrate the problems and the complexities parents encounter with birth, we briefly describe eight cases.

George, thirty-two, a clerk in a small store, had been prepared for the birth of his first baby by taking childbirth classes with his wife. The doula observed, however, that he looked out the window during most of the labor. The doula made many efforts to engage him in activities with the labor but was unsuccessful. After the birth George said to the doula with great feeling, "This has been the most wonderful experience of my life." The doulas realized at that moment that this father had done all he could do, which was right for him.

Tony, thirty-five, worked in computer technology when his first baby was born. Tony had grown up in a culture where fathers did not participate in delivery and where physical modesty in hospitals was very much respected. Although he had lived in the United States for many years and had taken childbirth classes, he reluctantly attended the birth. These parents had no doula. Six months after the delivery, he and his wife sought help for marital and sexual problems. After exploring some of his strong negative feelings, the father realized that he was very angry at his wife because he had a deep cultural belief that his wife should not be exposed in his presence in front of other men. He felt that physical exposure at birth verged on being almost pornographic, and he was personally humiliated. Intellectually he knew this was wrong, but emotionally he could not alter his response. Much distress and several therapy sessions were necessary to work this out. A number of fathers have reported variants of this problem. It is helpful to remember that for some men birth mixes sexuality and paternity in a sometimes confusing manner. Intimate involvement in the care of a woman in labor is not right for everyone.

Similarly another father, a twenty-three-year-old airline clerk who had been present for the birth of his first baby, said, "It was the worst thing that I had ever seen—to see my wife in that kind of pain." He felt that he had helped create this situation: "How can I have made her go through this pain?" But he also said that all fathers should be there to see their babies born and to understand what their wives go through. This couple did not have a doula.

A new mother, thirty-one, an accountant married to a lawyer, thirty-three, noted after the birth of their first baby: "We both didn't want any outside help, but I was lucky. There were no other deliveries on the floor at the time I came to the hospital, and the obstetric nurse was able to stay with me and my husband during the entire labor. I couldn't have done it without her. My husband was helpful, but the nurse was essential." In this case the nurse functioned as both a nurse and a doula.

A twenty-eight-year-old teacher in a day-care center had similar feelings. After the birth of her first baby, she said, "I couldn't have had the birth without the doula. The thing I wanted most from my husband was just that he hold my hand."

Another mother, thirty-five, experienced feelings of depression while facing her third pregnancy. Her husband, thirty-seven, worked in real estate. In uncovering the source of these feelings, she revealed how angry and abandoned she had felt because of her husband's passivity during the previous two births. She had wanted him to be more helpful, participative, and involved. He, on the other hand, had believed he was truly involved just by being there and by saying nice and encouraging things to her. He was surprised at her distressed feelings and did not know what more he could have done. We believe that the presence of a doula might have prevented this situation.

Another father, a twenty-nine-year-old physician, stated, "With our first baby I was so overcome emotionally that I could not make any rational observations about what was happening, and I truly believed there was imminent dan-

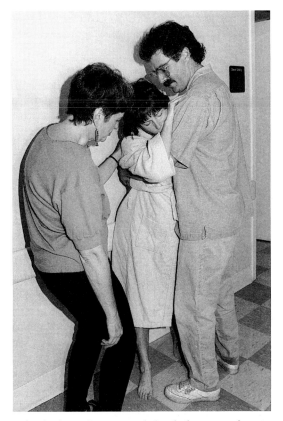

The doula is showing with her body posture how it will help if the woman lets herself sink into her husband's arms.

ger at every stage of labor." Again, this couple had no doula.

A thirty-five-year-old mother, married to a skilled carpenter in his thirties, wrote the following to us after the birth of their first baby: "The doula's support was effective and meaningful. She eased a great burden from my husband, as well as myself. She freed my husband up to be exactly where I needed him, when I needed him. My first response to having a doula was negative, my husband's positive. I must admit I did not like the idea of having a third person, a stranger, in on one of the most personal experiences of our lives. My husband felt he could use the support to keep him going in the right direction. The outcome of our experience is positive to both of us. The team of my husband and the doula kept me relaxed and focused. My husband was able to tend to my needs of touching and sharing, and the doula was able to coach me and encourage me at the same time. My husband felt this was a great help to him and let him be closer to me and stay relaxed."

The complexity of the father's role and the expectations given to the father in our society are illustrated by these couples. The wide variation in life experiences and cultural backgrounds makes any simple prescription for the role of fathers at birth impossible. Fathers and mothers need to know the difference in types of support that may be available to them during childbirth. This information could give them permission to make the appropriate choices that are best for their particular situation.

CAN A FATHER BE A DOULA?

We are frequently asked if a father can function as a doula. After all, he loves his wife and cares for her dearly, he has had childbirth classes and has learned what relieves pain for her, and he is especially sensitive to her needs. What if a father and mother believe anyone else present during the labor might interfere with the unique intimacy between them? "We want privacy; we want to have this experience for ourselves. My partner is going to help me, coach me."

When labor begins in earnest, many of these intentions fall away, and both mother and father are greatly relieved when a nurse remains and helps. We strongly believe that a father cannot be a doula for the mother. A father is rarely able, moment to moment, to appreciate what is happening with the mother and whether each change is a normal part of the actual events of labor. An easier role for him is to give emotional support to the mother while the doula is there to support them both through the labor.

Michel Odent, the pioneering French obstetrician, noted that certain men have a beneficial effect on labor, while the presence of others only slows it down.[30] As an example, he mentioned a particular father who acted overprotective and possessive, continually massaging and caressing his wife. Odent commented that "this father anticipated her demands rather than responding to them. The woman in labor required calm, but he could only provide stimulation." Men sometimes find it hard to observe, accept, and understand women's instinctive behavior during labor and delivery. Instead, they often try to keep laboring women from slipping out of a rational, self-controlled state.

The anxiety that accompanies labor causes some men to react in counterproductive ways. For example, the father may lose touch with the mother's emotional state as he becomes more anxious and feels a need to take control. Performance anxiety, overactivity, excessive talking, or passivity may also occur. Any of these reactions may be exactly the opposite of what the woman needs. The doula can help him be in better harmony with the mother's emotional state.

As labor progresses, even fathers experienced in childbirth and trained in classes will often leave the labor room for increasingly long periods of relief (to get coffee, make telephone calls, and so on). While other fathers remain, they may distance themselves from their wives as a result of their fears. These episodes can generate unconscious anger or disappointment for the mothers, because they, too, have bought into the belief that the fathers should be able to do everything. When a doula is available to both the man and the woman, they are able to fulfill their individual responsibilities: for the mother, going on with the birth, asking and receiving what she needs in the way of appropriate and em-

pathic responses; for the father, being as supportive as he can be, yet responding at his own level of comfort and competence without losing face.

A doula needs to be sensitive at all times to the couple's relationship. When all is progressing well and they are interacting successfully, she steps away and remains present but in the background. She also helps involve the father appropriately, for example, by showing him how to massage the mother's back.

Often the doula will have to take time out to support another family member. In one case we heard about, where the mother and father were doing quite well together, the mother-in-law broke down because the couple's first pregnancy had been a stillbirth. The doula's main role at that moment was to help the mother-in-law and to protect the mother from added stress.

If the father is the only support and labor is not progressing easily and ends in a cesarean section, the father may feel that he failed in his role as coach and failed his wife. This sense of failure and guilt may affect his self-esteem. Sometimes men and women unconsciously harbor feelings of guilt or anger toward each other or toward themselves when the outcome is not as they expected.

There are other potential risks to the relationship. For some fathers, a cesarean section exonerates them from guilt or failure, for they can consciously believe that it is their wives' fault: a disproportionate pelvis, for instance, and not their inability to be good coaches. A father may also become angry at the mother for not doing her part in what they were both taught. The reality might, however, have been a dysfunctional labor. Such feelings can be prevented or ameliorated with support from an experienced doula. The doula can help both parents understand the need for a cesarean section and feel positive about the safe outcome for their baby.

A birth happens in the context of an ongoing relationship, which can be complex. A father may be struggling unconsciously with unresolved issues of mortality, sexuality, identification with the birth process, paternity, and confusion about his role.

So many variables of an emotional nature can be projected into the birth situation. In contrast, the doula's role remains relatively constant. She is there only as a supportive and informed birth assistant. Women who choose to become doulas want to help other women and have a certain empathic sense of childbirth. They have an opportunity during their training to understand their own personal issues associated with childbirth, and they learn not to project onto the laboring woman their own emotional needs. (See Appendix A in regard to the training of a doula.)

The experienced doula knows when to be a strong presence and support as well as when to sit quietly by as the woman moves into her own body process. It is easier for the doula than for the father to shift from a guiding, directing, or suggesting role to a quieter, encouraging role, or to any other role needed as the events and drama of labor shift and change. Such a shift can be difficult for a father's self-esteem. Like the father's role, the doula's is not medical, but her experience with birth gives her a comfort and a knowledge about labor that can be extremely useful. She can be the interface between the woman or the couple and the medical staff as she applies her skills and sensitivity throughout the long hours of labor.

HELPING A FATHER PARTICIPATE

The presence of a doula complements a father's role and strengthens it. A doula often can give suggestions and encourage the father to touch, to talk, and to help in ways that feel truly comfortable to him and comforting to the mother. In conversation with the authors, Dr. Martin Greenberg, an expert on fathers and author of *Birth of a Father*, has commented:

The doula stays in the background and respects the couple's moment of affection.

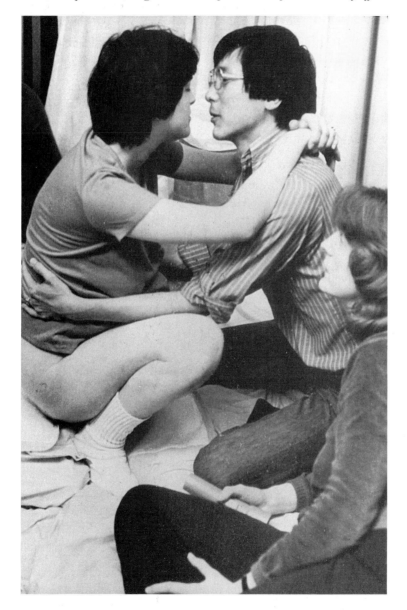

The mother has a biologically based task which is driven by a time clock, while the father feels like he is floating in air without a connection, uncertain about his tasks. A support person during this time can reach out to both of them, decrease the father's anxiety, give him support and encouragement, and teach him specific tasks, allowing him to reach out to his wife in a more caring and nurturing fashion.

Over and over again women say that "just knowing my husband was there, just his holding my hand, was the most important thing for me—while I could trust the doula's words and actions and let myself go, feeling safe that her experience would see us through."

An analogy that helps to clarify the distinction between the doula's and the father's role is the acceptance by the medical profession of the fact that doctors cannot objectively treat or care for their own families. Their strong emotional involvement leads them to judgments about diagnosis and therapy that they would not make with other patients.

Fathers, with the support of the doula, should be able to participate at any level that feels right and natural for them. In this way they can experience fully the joy and wonder of watching their babies come into the world. For father and mother, birth can then be a truly shared event—mutually moving, inspiring, and loving.

6

. . .

ENHANCING THE
BIRTH EXPERIENCE

. . .

*I get them to sleep between contractions by talking very softly
and saying "You're doing fine, keep it up, you can do it,
we'll be together, I'm here with you." I always keep my
hand on them. Then they go to sleep.*

A DOULA

· · · AFTER CHOOSING A DOULA, a couple will find it especially helpful to have two or three visits with her well before labor begins, as mentioned in Chapter 2. These visits with the doula in a relaxed setting in their home permit the parents to discuss their expectations and make plans for labor and delivery. Parents have found this process valuable because they may not yet have shared with each other their personal wishes, thoughts, or feelings about labor and delivery. The visit with the doula creates an occasion to discuss these issues, and the doula adds her encouragement.

EARLY CONTACT WITH THE DOULA

An experienced doula will be familiar with the regulations of individual hospitals and the protocols of obstetricians. She may also be knowledgeable about the advantages and limitations of the different caregiving settings. It is extremely valuable to learn about these beforehand rather than in the midst of labor, when couples may learn that parts of their long-desired plans are not permitted and then may have their hopes dashed. For example, the hospital may insist on every mother having continuous fetal monitoring and staying in bed.

Mothers who feel it is important (as we do) to be free to walk during labor need to know this regulation beforehand, to discuss it with their doctor or midwife, and, if necessary, change to a more flexible hospital.

By discussing their individual goals and various choices in advance, parents gain time to work out their options with their physician. Parents face many choices regarding labor, delivery, and the time afterwards. Not every hospital or birth center can provide them all, so parents may have to be flexible and to consider which are the most important arrangements. The doula can help them define their objectives. Childbirth education will also help in learning what to expect and how to prepare and plan. A doula by no means replaces such preparation. Couples may find that childbirth classes leave them with many questions about, for instance, the films shown, ways to evaluate the options discussed, or the effectiveness of relaxation and imagery techniques.

Meetings with the doula are the time to review step-by-step what will happen during labor and childbirth, and what the doula will be doing. In this way the couple can become familiar with the procedures while getting to know the doula. During these discussions, parents may on rare occasions find that they are not compatible with this particular woman. If that should be the case, they should make this clear and start looking for another doula more in rhythm with their personalities and styles.

With the selected doula a mother can actually practice various positions for labor and rehearse relaxation, breathing, and visualization techniques to help reduce pain and to work through the contractions. This is a good time for the woman to tell the doula about what helps her reduce discomfort when she has pain. While acknowledging this valuable information, the doula can help the mother realize that those techniques may need to change completely during labor. A doula must be able to change with the mother's needs, and the mother must learn to feel safe enough to express her changing needs to both the doula and the father.

EARLY LABOR AND THE DOULA

We have found it helpful for the mother to have the doula come to her home sometime during labor. For some mothers it is helpful for the doula to come there at the beginning of labor, and then to remain in contact either by phone or in person. The exact nature of early labor for the individual mother will determine the timing. It is crucial to provide appropriate support at appropriate times—not too early and not so

The father and doula working together in early labor.

shortened. Often mothers expecting their first baby rush to the hospital too early in labor and miss out on the benefits of having most of the labor at home. It is not unusual for a mother who has been experiencing some contractions all night to arrive at the hospital and still be at two to three centimeters dilatation. Of course, the final decision to go to the hospital will be made by the woman and her doctor or the birth facility.

In the beginning of labor the cervix is thinning and beginning to open. Early labor can be a time for a woman to begin

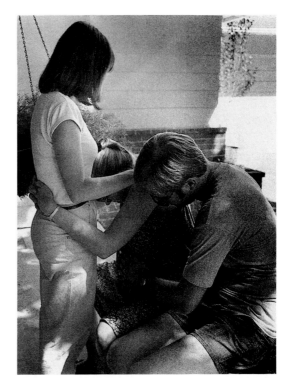

much as to overwhelm the family. Knowing the doula will be available anytime during labor lessens the parents' initial anxiety, and the couple can then remain at home longer with more productive labor and less pain. When the mother is being supported at home and relaxing in a familiar environment, this early, or latency, phase of labor may be to work with her body. Having practiced techniques in advance with the doula, the mother may feel more confident and empowered, able to trust her own ability to flow with and handle the early contractions. The time spent preparing reinforces this confidence. It is helpful for women to be supported in a way that enables them to tap into their own strength and resources. A doula can help the mother determine whether she is in real labor and not just having the so-called Braxton-Hicks contractions, which are a normal part of late pregnancy. (See also Chapter 7 in regard to the diagnosis of labor.)

Most mothers progress more rapidly in familiar surroundings, using comfort measures for relaxation learned in advance or suggested by the doula. During this period mothers have found the following suggestions helpful:

1. Walk as much as possible because this appears to shorten labor and reduce pain.

2. If the membranes are not ruptured, take a warm bath, which can help you remain more relaxed. If the membranes are ruptured, a shower is preferable due to the risk of infection.

3. Change positions at least every half hour.

4. Drink plenty of liquids (fruit juices, soup) and light foods if recommended by your doctor. Urinate frequently.

(See Appendix A for additional detailed instructions for mother, father, and doula.)

LATE LABOR AND THE DOULA

Once the mother is at the hospital with labor progressing toward full dilatation of the cervix and delivery near, the following signs may be noted:

1. Flushing of the face and body
2. An increase in bloody mucus
3. Longer and stronger contractions with little rest in between
4. Legs often becoming shaky
5. A feeling of nausea
6. Feeling of an urge to push

The mother, father, doula, and medical staff often then work as a team, using techniques that are most helpful. In the transition period when labor is most intense, and then when the cervix is fully dilated, the encouraging support of the doula becomes especially helpful. At those times the mother often believes she cannot make it through another contraction, and the father often experiences his most intense distress, feeling helpless at relieving the woman's discomfort. At this point the doula's support can give the mother the incentive to continue: the doula sometimes holds the woman, she reminds the mother (and the father) over and over again that she can continue and is doing great, and

she helps the mother breathe through those last powerful contractions. A thirty-three-year-old woman, Polly, describing the birth of her third baby, said, "Bill was great, just great—but when I was losing it, I couldn't have done it without Virginia [the doula]!"

When necessary, if there is a change during the course of the labor, the doula will help parents redefine their objectives. The doula can help ensure that parents are informed about everything that is happening, step-by-step. When

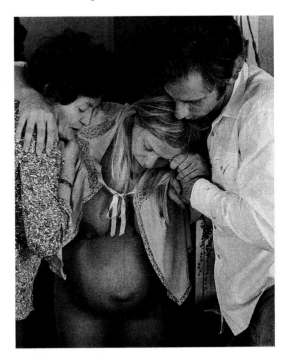

In late labor the mother is held first by the doula and then by her own mother and husband.

women know what is happening, they begin to realize that progress is being made and that there is an end in sight. If progress is too slow for some reason, they need to know what can and will be done. As Drs. Kierin O'Driscoll and Declan Meagher of Dublin, whose work we describe in the next chapter, point out, everyone attending a woman in la-

sition often finds it very helpful both to focus on the doula's face while breathing through a contraction and to hold the father's hand.

Sometimes during labor something may upset a mother's sense of security. For example, she may not fully understand why a medication or procedure was given and may wonder if this means

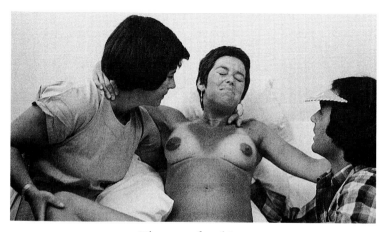

The onset of pushing.

bor "has a responsibility to ensure that [she] genuinely understands the purpose of every medical procedure and the results of every examination."

As we said before, it is important for the mother to tell the doula which techniques particularly help in relieving pain, since each mother responds differently. The doula can then individualize her care. For instance, a woman in tran-

that something has gone wrong. It is critical that the nurse, the physician, or the doula discuss this with the mother, to answer her questions, clarify her condition, and relieve her concern.

During this experience both the mother and the father may be stirred in ways they did not expect. Old fears, loneliness, and dependency needs may be triggered. Tearfulness may occur.

They both may be helped by holding each other. Excretions, sounds, sights, smells, cries, or screams may trigger old memories of hospitalizations or elicit other unexpected reactions. Many times men feel dizzy and sick and need to leave for a short while to regain calm and control, after which they can return. With a doula present, this is not a problem.

At the end of the delivery, after certain vital assessments are made, the doctor, the nurses, and the doula leave both parents alone with the baby so the new family can get to know each other. Doulas can help parents insist on and protect this time. The infant is in an unusually alert state after birth. All sensory systems are operative, and the baby is particularly responsive.[20] Such an alert state seems programmed by nature so that newborns are ready to meet their parents, and parent and infant can begin to "take each other in" and become acquainted. Newborns often respond to their parents' voices at this early age.

The next day the doula visits both parents to debrief them on the labor and go over the labor and birth experience. Surprisingly, many mothers and fathers are concerned that they did something wrong, when actually their behavior has been absolutely normal and they have managed very well. It helps to go over all the details and be reinformed and reassured about the birth. (See Chapter 8 regarding a continuing role for the doula after birth.)

Few other events in the life of a couple bring them together in such a memorable and complex fashion. The strong need of both parents to be cared for during this momentous and demanding event may well be matched by an unusual receptivity. The presence of a nurturing, encouraging person throughout this entire intense experience may have both a conscious and a subliminal effect. In reassuring the parents and enhancing their sense of accomplishment, the doula may be modeling the parental role for them—mothering the mother and parenting the parents. As Professor Johnny Lind of Karolinska Hospital in Stockholm put it: "The family is born in the delivery room."

7

. . .

THE DUBLIN EXPERIENCE

. . .

*Women in general have . . . [much] to gain from the presence
of a female companion who is not just sympathetic but is
informed as well, and therefore in a much better position
to provide the sense of firm reassurance which is so sorely
needed at this time.*

DRS. KIERIN O'DRISCOLL
AND DECLAN MEAGHER, 1986[31]

. . . "YOU'RE GREAT—YOU'RE doing well. That's right, relax. Breathe easily—breathe out through the contraction like this." In a soft voice, leaning close to the mother, a hand ever present on her arm or abdomen, the nurse-midwife continues: "That's good. Breathe out, like this—good—look at me." The midwife guides the mother through, speaking slowly in rhythm with the out breath. "Look at me. That's good, that's it. Breathe out. Let it go—out. It's easing now. Yes, good—you're marvelous."

The words of this nurse-midwife capture the warm, devoted care women in labor receive at the National Maternity Hospital in Dublin, Ireland. We traveled to Dublin to observe this care because we had heard of the extraordinarily good results—in terms of length of labor, use of anesthesia, and cesarean-section rates—that this hospital has shown.

The major emphasis of the obstetricians at the National Maternity Hospital is on the one-to-one personal attention of the nurse, and we wished to see how similar this was to support by a doula. As the innovators of the so-called active management of labor, Drs. Kierin O'Driscoll and Declan Meagher note:

Mere physical presence is not enough, the nurse must appreciate that her primary duty to the mother is to provide the emotional support so badly needed at this critical time and not simply to record vital signs in a detached clinical manner. A guarantee is given to every expectant woman who attends this hospital that she will have a personal nurse through the whole labor, from the time of her admission to after her baby is born without regard to the hour of day or night.

THE PREVENTION OF PROLONGED LABOR

Interviewing Dr. Kierin O'Driscoll, we found a wiry, intense, enthusiastic, energetic man. Early in his career he began to question why dystocia (arrested labor) would arise in perfectly normal women after they came into the hospital. In the 1950s labors often lasted seventy-two hours or longer. Why did this prolongation of labor happen to normal women with a single fetus? He also observed that no one ever knew exactly when labor started. He began to observe what helped a woman in labor and what practices led to prolonged labor. His primary goal was the prevention of prolonged labor. By 1972 he had reduced normal labor of a first-time mother to no more than twelve hours.

Dr. O'Driscoll explained that some of the key factors included proper diagnosis of labor, one-to-one care, touch, and special treatment for first-time mothers. "If you look after primiparous (first-time) mothers properly they will deliver themselves next time. If not, they could be made an obstetrical cripple for the rest of their life." Birth, he pointed out, must preserve a woman's dignity, and must remain a joyous event with a woman feeling in command of herself. When he began practice, women were left screaming or were put asleep. In the United States the problem of dystocia has been solved surgically: a 9 percent cesarean-section rate in 1970, 20 percent in 1980, and 30 percent in 1990.

The standard of nursing in the National Maternity Hospital includes exceptional caring and good humor. The nurses are trained to touch the mother, to have eye and hand contact, to use the *en face* position (nurse and mother eye-to-eye in the same horizontal plane). Dr. O'Driscoll goes on to explain:

As we began to understand and made a more rational approach to contain labor, we found we needed to change the organization of the labor ward, giving every woman a midwife to monitor her labor closely. This began to result in shorter and shorter labors. We found

The mother feels safe with the nurse-midwife.

that we could deliver 225 babies [a year] for every midwife (where before it was 95 babies per midwife). So for every 200 deliveries we needed one less midwife.

The "charge midwife" (called sister) and the consultant physician are colleagues. All others, including the other doctors, answer to this midwife in charge. Midwives in Ireland have a different status than do those in the United States. The Irish midwife has a complementary role, not competing with the physicians. The physicians are consultants to the sister and are very respectful; there is no suspicion or antipathy.

Dr. O'Driscoll explained that another key factor is the education of the patient:

this is education in the truest sense. The antenatal education teaches the mother to understand the process—what happens when she is in labor, how the labor graph used in that hospital works, how to help herself, and how to gain confidence in the support she will receive.

This system, which differs from that in the United States, vividly illustrates the potent effects of continuous emotional support. This model is currently under intensive study in several hospitals in the United States. In U.S. hospitals the supportive function of the Dublin nurse-midwife could be provided by a doula.

The active management of labor began with the express purpose of reducing the length of labor and thereby its

The midwife aligns her face with the mother's (en face) and holds her for full support.

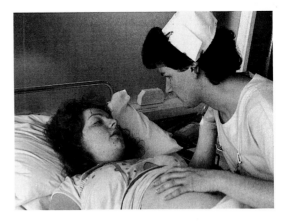

Walking in labor.

complications, and it is a comprehensive way of thinking about and facilitating the entire labor and delivery experience for a woman and her partner. It includes understanding the progress of her labor, her family history and number of pregnancies, and the complete organization of her experience in the hospital. Managing the labor in a thoughtfully orchestrated way allows the woman to feel attended to at all times—allows her to feel that she will be able to handle her labor, that she will

be safe, that her dignity and experience matter, and that her body's responses are natural and normal.

THE DIAGNOSIS OF LABOR

The obstetricians at the National Maternity Hospital emphasize that the active management of labor requires a complete understanding of the *diagnosis of labor*. A woman is either in labor or not in labor: the clear-cut criteria are known by the midwife in charge, who examines each woman. The childbirth education program also educates the woman to recognize true signs of labor. If a woman comes in having contractions or believing she may be in labor, but examination reveals that she is not in labor (20 percent of women who present to the delivery ward are not in labor), she will be sent to stay for a day in the antenatal ward, where she may go into labor at a later time, or be sent home the next day to wait until labor begins. In this hospital labor is very rarely induced.

When the diagnosis of labor is made, each woman is assigned her personal nurse-midwife, usually a nurse who is training to become a midwife and who will remain with her throughout labor. Each mother is assured that she will deliver within twelve hours, or in rare cases, shortly afterward. In this hospital, 50 percent of the first-time (primiparous) mothers have babies in five or fewer hours, and 90 percent of primiparous mothers have babies in under eight hours. A few first-time mothers (less than 2 percent) have babies at twelve hours or a very short time thereafter.

A diagnosis of labor is made if a woman has been having strong and regular contractions every eight to ten minutes that last thirty to forty-four seconds each, if her cervix is dilated and thinned out (effaced), and if she has a bloody mucous show. The latter alone is not sufficient to diagnose labor, nor are contractions alone (since they may be Braxton-Hicks contractions). Only when she is diagnosed as being in labor does the "counting" or measurement of her labor progress begin.

This is not just a matter of labeling. If labor is incorrectly diagnosed and the measurement of labor begins too soon, a misperception of "labor lasting for hours and hours" is accepted. In that situation women will feel overwhelmed and out of control, and their anxious caregivers may feel compelled to initiate obstetric interventions such as oxytocin to increase uterine contractions. One thing can lead to another, and the mother can often end up many hours later with a cesarean section. Had the diagnosis been made correctly, she could have returned home and rested, knowing that the sensations she felt were not yet true labor. One to ten days later she would go into actual labor and most likely would have a natural delivery.

We have gone over this description of the diagnosis of labor in some detail because we think this is a critical element in the National Maternity Hospital's management of birth. If labor has indeed started but the mother's cervix is not dilating at a rate of at least one centimeter per hour, first-time mothers (only) will be given oxytocin after a number of hours. Only 30 percent of primiparous mothers are given oxytocin. (In U.S. hospitals the percentage of women receiving oxytocin varies widely.) The active management of labor may also include rupturing the membranes (the "bag of waters") once the baby's head is engaged appropriately, if the membranes have not ruptured spontaneously.

ONE-TO-ONE CARE

The active management of labor has spread to many parts of Europe. Unfortunately, in most hospitals the one-to-one nursing component has been left out. Judging from our research, this is a fundamental error. These hospitals have not appreciated the importance of this continuous care in easing and shortening labor. We suspect that this particular ingredient of the program—the presence at all times of a caregiving nurse (or midwife or doula)—has the greatest influence on a successful outcome. As we saw in Chapter 3, in our studies we have been able to demonstrate almost the same results using *only* the component of a woman giving continuous emotional support. In the National Maternity Hospital in Dublin, birthing is women's work. Women caring for women continue an age-old tradition. The midwife practices her craft with skill, caring, and intuitive and experienced knowledge.

Drs. O'Driscoll and Meagher designed the active management of labor based on their perceptive observations of a large number of women experiencing the old style of "hospital labor." In that period in Dublin before 1967 a woman in labor was often alone and was not carefully checked, and labor could last a long time. "It was sometimes chaos, with no one knowing when the woman had started her labor; sometimes a woman was in bed for days without any sense of management or containment." They believed that this was inhumane and that if each woman could be helped by another woman from the beginning to the end of her labor, her outcome could be quite different. They saw labor as a natural event and believed that the earlier hospital system disrupted this natural process. They also observed an imbalance in the use of personnel. For example, many more nurses were available during the day, and only a skeletal crew was on duty at night.

Keeping in mind the necessity of providing one-to-one care for each mother, these doctors created teams, each consisting of a charge midwife, two senior midwives, and five student midwives. To help them understand the process of labor, medical and nursing students who rotated through the labor ward would also be put to work providing the same kind of continuous support on day or night shifts. Being quite aware of the differences between a primiparous mother and a multiparous mother, Keirin O'Driscoll created a two-color chart system so that everyone on the floor (including the maintenance people) would know whether each mother was having her first baby or a subsequent one.

With these approaches as a guide, graduate nurses in training for midwifery are now the main supportive persons for a mother throughout her labor. These nurses are the model for care and instruct the medical students and beginning nursing students in the techniques, manner, and attitudes useful while attending labor and delivery. Obstetricians and other physicians respect the role and importance of the midwife.

After the midwife in charge determines that a woman is in labor, she assigns a nurse-midwife to the mother, and the work of support begins. The father is welcomed in whatever level of involvement he wants. He is encouraged to be present at all times, to feel comfortable about taking a break, or to leave while an intervention takes place if he wishes. He is not put in the role of being the main support. It is clear that he is there as an emotional support, but not as an expert in facilitating labor. The nurse-midwife's focus is on the mother, but she is respectful toward the father; the nurse has him sit next to her and hold the mother's hand as the contrac-

tions get harder. She also asks him to hold the mother's arm while walking— the nurse-midwife on one side, the father on the other. The nurse-midwife works with the mother through each contraction, whether the mother is walking or remaining in bed. She says, "Tell me when you start having a pain." The nurse-midwives' continuous presence has an innate relaxing effect. A mother said: "I couldn't have done it without the nurse. When my husband started looking green, I sent him out for coffee. The most important thing for me was looking at the nurse's face, listening to her, holding her hand. My own sister was so nervous that I couldn't look at her. The nurse got me through it."

When the mother has a contraction while walking (as mentioned before, walking greatly helps accelerate dilatation of the cervix in early labor), the nurse-midwife has her lean against a wall, sigh out, let herself get loose, and focus her attention outward. Quietly guiding the mother through the contraction with relaxation breathing, the nurse-midwife reminds her to look at the nurse-midwife's face or at something in the hall. Focusing outward is a way for the woman to distance herself from focusing only on the pain. This attention to her natural breathing process, with focus on the exhalation, is different from any structured technique such as

Lamaze. Every fifteen minutes during the walking, the nurse-midwife helps the mother return to bed to listen to the baby's heartbeat. Whatever the nurse-midwife does, she informs the mother beforehand, and while proceeding: what she is going to do and why, and what the results are, in simple language. For example, "I'm going to listen to the baby's heart." She waits until after a contraction to press on the abdomen with the fetoscope to listen). "The heartbeat is perfect, strong—a healthy, normal rate of 140 beats. I'm going to time this contraction now: Good, you're doing great—nice and strong. Breathe it out—good; let it go. You're really great."

The nurse-midwives use different methods of managing pain or discomfort. The most frequently used and reinforced approach is the relaxation, exhaling, and focusing as just described. The nurse-midwife responds to a woman's questions about pain medications and informs her that she can have Demerol two times (fifty milligrams each time)

Stopping for a contraction.

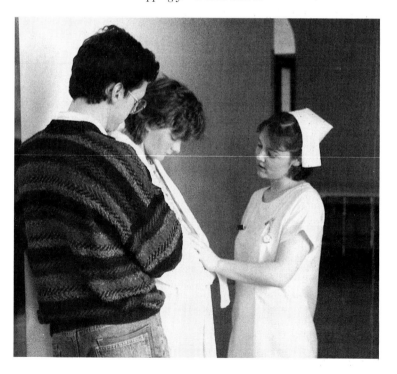

up to the time her cervix is dilated to six centimeters. There is also a mask with nitrous oxide (laughing gas) or, if the mother is very distressed and unable to cope, an epidural anesthetic. The nurse most often helps the mother work through the pain. Twenty percent of women select an epidural. The nurse-midwives praise the mother throughout labor, whatever the choice. Even though there is a great deal of praise, what we heard always seemed appropriate and genuine. As labor progresses and transition, at eight to ten centimeters, occurs, the nurse becomes even more intensely involved, helping the woman manage the power of the contractions. She may hold her close and face-to-face. She will continue to talk the mother through the contraction, reminding her again and again of breathing out and letting go, and telling her how great she is doing.

Within the first two days of observing at the National Maternity Hospital in Dublin, we met one couple having a first baby, one couple with one baby at home, another with two babies at home, another with three other children, another with seven other children, and one family who had had a stillbirth with their first child. In each case the fathers were trying to be as supportive as they could. The father would sit in a chair next to the mother (the nurse-midwife would be standing at the head of the bed quite close to the mother). Typically, the father had frightened eyes, a worried look, and sweating, clammy hands. He usually held the mother's hand. The mother would squeeze the father's hand as she had a contraction; that was important for her. After one-half to one hour or so, the father in some cases went out for a break. Some felt more comfortable leaving whenever there was an internal examination of the mother. Although most of these fathers had been through labor before and, except for one family, had had good outcomes, they would tense up as the mothers had pain. If left alone for a few minutes, they would feel unsure of how to help. Afterward, they all echoed what one father said: "I was really worried. You know, you don't know how things will go. It's a blessing, really, the baby's okay and my wife." One mother of two children, now having her third, said, "I hope Paddy doesn't come before the baby's born. He always makes me more nervous than I am."

A BIRTH AT THE NATIONAL MATERNITY HOSPITAL

The following scene was typical of many we observed. The mother and father arrive at the hospital. The mother has been having contractions, and she thinks she is in labor. The midwife in charge greets her, helps her get comfortable, puts her in the examining room, and invites the father to come in or wait in the waiting room. As the mother has a contraction, the midwife gently but clearly starts her guiding instructions, even before examining the mother. "Lie on your side, breathe in through your nose, and long slow breaths out through your mouth. Keep your eyes open; look at me—good, keep doing that, nice and slowly, that's good (she models for her). Purse your lips, make a swish sound as you breathe out—good. Take a big breath in through your nose, keep your eyes open—look at the window or at my face, blow and release, breathe out through your mouth. Again; now look at me—keeps your mind off pain. That's right, you're doing great, you're doing marvelous. What time did the pain start?" The mother says she had pains all night. "Did you sleep?" She dozed. "Was there a bloody show?" Yesterday, she indicates. "How much blood? Show me in my hand." The midwife explains everything before she does it. "I'm going to examine you to see if you're in labor. If you are, I'm going to break the bag of waters to check the color of the water and to accelerate the labor. Okay? Tell me when you are getting a pain. Now I'll set you up and tell you what's happening." (She has checked the mother's pulse, blood pressure, and tem-

perature.) She examines the mother. "You're in labor—three centimeters, a very good start. I haven't broken the waters yet because the baby's head is not yet down. I want you to walk for one hour. Walking helps get the head down. Walk with your husband and nurse now. The best way to get the baby's head down is by walking. Then it'll be very quick. I think you'll have a short labor. I'll examine you later." She introduces the mother to her personal nurse-midwife.

The three of them proceed slowly up and down the corridor. The nurse-midwife almost always has her hand on the mother. It is quiet, peaceful, and calm. They pass a similar trio. The nurse-midwife says, "Tell me when you feel a contraction starting—we'll stop and I'll help you through it." The woman says, "Yes, now." They stop; the nurse-midwife suggests that the woman lean easily against the wall, and she helps her through the contraction. The time passes quickly in this fashion: they walk, they listen, and as contractions get stronger or the mother feels any change or wants to get in bed, the nurse-midwife follows at the mother's pace: staying with her for every moment of the experience, reassuring, validating, comforting, appropriately respecting the father's position, and being the stable presence of experience and confidence for both the mother and the father.

The midwife in charge comes periodically throughout the labor to help the training nurse-midwife who is providing support. She checks what is happening, reassures the mother, and at appropriate times checks for dilatation.

children may say, "I can't do it. No, it's really too hard—I can't do it!" At this point, both midwives help the woman in pushing the baby out, with the charge midwife reminding the mother how to push through the contraction, but only

a

The following six photographs were taken within five minutes late in labor.

As the second stage gets under way (when the cervix is fully dilated and the head is descending), many women sometimes lose their sense of direction and control. They feel overwhelmed and even after having delivered several

when she feels like pushing. Here is an excellent example of how this intense one-to-one communication is essential. The nurse-midwife says softly, "Just one person talking so as not to cause distraction. We're going to make use of that contraction. When it comes, let's use your own power to push this baby out. Good, good, take a big breath—no talk or sound. Put your chin on your chest and push that breath into your bottom as long as you can hold it, then quickly two more times within this contraction. In three contractions you're going to push that baby right out. I can see its hair—great, good, you're doing great."

"Now, rest in between contractions." She helps the woman into position. Sometimes the mother gets leverage by holding her own knees, or the two midwives let the mother push her feet against them to brace herself. It was unusual to us to see such close physical contact—so much more humane than the old stirrups. The woman either sits up in the bed, as high as possible, or is on her left side. The midwives often use a bed-wedge pillow behind her back.

As the contraction starts, the nurse-midwife reminds the mother: "We're going to make the best use of this pushing energy. Now another contraction: take a big breath, mouth closed, chin on chest, and push into your bottom and forward. Hold the breath as long as possible. Good, now a second big breath. Good, go along with the urge to push. Now a third big breath—good, push into your bottom, and stay forward. Good, good, the baby's come forward a lot.

You're great. Now rest. Let me know when the urge to push starts—that first push is the best push. Good." She has the father stand just behind the mother with his arm around her shoulders, letting him support the mother as she pushes. The midwives recognize the mother's incredible need for encouragement in order to keep going. Even when any of the team or family is tired, the midwives keep going cheerfully, reminding the mother that she has all the power she needs to push the baby out and that she's feeling pressure now, not pain. When the head has crowned, the midwives guide the mother gently to relax and look at the focal point, just breathing in a light and slow breath to let her body do the rest of the natural pushing out of the baby.

A MODEL OF HUMANE CARE

Sitting as quiet observers in the corner of the room for an extended period, we saw an entire system geared toward supporting the mother and father through their baby's birth—without anxiety and with gentle caring, encouragement, warmth, and displays of real affection. Never in the entire week, after attending forty deliveries, did we hear any mother spoken to, or about, gruffly. The mothers were treated with unusual sensitivity. We saw a warmth develop between the nurse-midwife and each mother—a component we think is extremely valuable. The mother is held both physically and emotionally. Every caregiver seemed aware that this was a very special time for each couple, and each mother was treated as a special individual, whether the mother was sad, grumpy, or upset. The equanimity of the nurses and midwives is a valuable model for all obstetrics. The cycle of nurturing and empowerment that occurs in this process makes a woman feel valued and enhances her self-esteem. If an extra nurse met a mother even for a few minutes, for example, while delivering something to her room, she would come back after the delivery, if she could, and ask, "What did you have—a girl or boy? That's great—congratulations!"

c

b

The whole system used accurate and appropriate observations of fetal heartbeat, maternal blood pressure, uterine contractability, and, only when necessary, fetal scalp sampling and fetal monitoring. Modern medical care, humanism, and warmth were balanced in the proper proportions, without overreliance on high-technology interventions to manage labor.

As we mentioned earlier, many of the units in the world that purport to employ the active management of labor use the same definition of labor, rupture the membranes, and use oxytocin, but they disregard what we consider an essential ingredient of the method—the personal nurse. This personal one-to-one care is so naturally ingrained in the personnel of the National Maternity Hospital that

d

alone in labor day or night, and that everything is geared toward that goal. This important message is a powerful subliminal suggestion, in itself helping to bring about a short, normal labor.

Another important achievement at this Dublin hospital is the unusually low

e

they themselves may not appreciate its immense value and may not have emphasized this ingredient of care when teaching or explaining the active management method to visitors from abroad. Since rupturing of the membranes appears to shorten labor by thirty to ninety minutes, and only about 30 percent of the mothers receive oxytocin, the one-to-one midwifery care accounts for much of the remarkable results at this hospital.

Visiting several of the classes, we saw how the childbirth educators—experienced midwives who have worked closely in the system—cheerfully and warmly help the mothers prepare for labor. The whole emphasis is on assuring the mother that her labor will be under twelve hours, that she will never be left

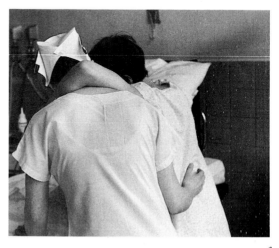

f

complication rate for both the mother and the baby. During the past fifteen years the cesarean-section rate has varied from only 5 to 6 percent, and the mean length of labor for first-time mothers is slightly less than six hours. At the same time, the statistics on the health of the babies delivered continues to be most impressive. The low cesarean-section rate at the National Maternity Hospital raises many questions about the high cesarean-section rate in many parts of the United States.[31]

In summary, our observation period at the National Maternity Hospital vividly demonstrated how significant every component of care and organization is in normalizing the birth experience. Theirs is a unique model that can help us all in reducing the complications of labor and in making delivery of a baby an easier, healthier, and more joyous experience.

8

. . .

SUPPORT AFTER BIRTH

. . .

A mother . . . finds it very hard to give up the nurses' care of her, and to be left alone to care for her infant in the very way that she herself needs to be treated.

D. W. WINNICOTT,
Babies and Their Mothers [40]

· · · AS WE SAW IN CHAPTER 3, the effects of doula support during labor continue after the birth. The study done in Johannesburg found that mothers with a doula in labor had increased feelings of self-confidence, felt they had managed labor and delivery well, and were more involved with their babies immediately after birth. They also noted that mothers without a doula had a decrease in their self-esteem between delivery and six weeks postpartum, while the women who had a doula during labor had an increase in self-esteem during that same period. Most importantly, at six weeks the doula-supported mothers had a much lower score in measures of depression than women who had no doula during labor. Measures of anxiety were also reduced in the mothers who had received support. The doula-supported mothers had increased success with breast-feeding, plus a more positive attitude toward both their infants and the fathers. Interestingly, the infants of these mothers had significantly fewer feeding problems.

There is a remarkable similarity between the results of doula support in the South African study and the behavior of mothers given early and increased contact with their newborn infants (the so-called bonding studies). Both groups of mothers showed or reported increased affection and attention to their babies, had an increased desire to stay home and

care for their infants in the first weeks, and were more likely to pick up their babies whenever there was crying. These mothers also tended to breast-feed more often and longer. Such striking differences six weeks later from such a short period of support is a reminder that the period of labor is a time when the mother is especially sensitive to environmental factors and open to learning and growth.[22]

THE NEED FOR SUPPORT AFTER DELIVERY

The need for support does not, of course, stop at the moment of birth. When first-time parents come home from the hospital with their new infant, they embark on a task for which they have little preparation or experience. While almost all societies have a system for helping parents through this period, the United States sadly has lost the customs and arrangements that once had this effect. At present the lack of a widely accepted cultural tradition for giving the necessary support to families after childbirth is a major deficiency. In the past a mother's mother and other female relatives provided this assistance and guidance. But today the mother's mother is often at work and there may be no one to fill the void.

It is often difficult for a new mother to recognize her needs and feelings and give herself permission to ask for help. Usually neither parent has a good understanding of the needs of a young infant and therefore cannot anticipate the endless demands of a newborn child. To shift from an active life where a mother has had social and work contacts with a large number of friendly and supportive associates to meeting the never-ending demands of a young infant is a momentous change. The burden of continuous responsibility with no letup and the unusual and unexpected degree of fatigue can make a mother feel desperate about whether she can survive and how she will manage.

During the first days after the birth of a baby, the mother is experiencing major physical and hormonal changes. When first-time mothers routinely spent four to five days in the hospital (more in earlier decades), the entire hospital staff was familiar with the reactions of mothers and their needs and set up classes to prepare them for the care of the babies at home. "Baby blues" on the second or third day postpartum were expected. Usually a mother had passed through this period before taking her baby home.

Now mothers go home the next day, or perhaps in two days, after giving birth. In our work with new parents it has always been surprising how little of what we told mothers the day of delivery was understood and retained. Even though they appeared to hear and understand and sometimes asked appropriate questions, a day or two later it would be as if the subject had never been discussed. We learned to save our explanations until later. This lapse of memory was due to the exceptional physical and emotional demands on the mother during labor and in the early hours after delivery which made it impossible for her to process the directions that were being provided.

Nowadays, the task of adequately preparing parents for the care of their baby is formidable. There is no time for mothers to establish a satisfying interaction and learn to breast-feed their babies in a safe, supportive environment before being discharged. Concerns about jaundice and the behavior of the baby may not be resolved before the infant goes home. Explanations and instructions by the nurses and pediatrician, as well as group discussions among mothers, which could give a mother a reasonable degree of confidence about her ability to manage her baby no longer take place.

Even in the days of longer hospital stays, the transition to independent par-

asked a large number of mothers to comment on any problems during the postnatal stay in the hospital. Almost every mother answered, "I have not had time to get to know my baby, and to know what to do with my baby at home." The leaders of our maternity

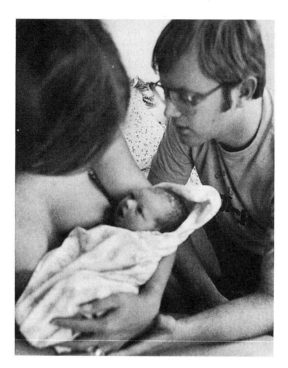

enthood was still difficult. When they returned home, mothers who felt in control in the hospital were often overwhelmed by a situation that made them feel helpless. Suddenly the baby was dictating or controlling their lives.

As part of our research, we recently

· · ·

Each of the photographs from this chapter

onward are of families you saw

during their labor.

· · ·

unit report that currently the hospital is receiving a large number of telephone requests for classes to help new parents learn about caring for their babies. This is not surprising, since the vast majority of first-time parents have had no experience with a young infant. We have seen that new mothers who have cared for younger siblings or have baby-sat young infants usually know how to handle the common problems of infants and generally feel somewhat confident in the early care of the infant.

After a mother has a baby, her mind tends to go back to an early time in her life, and many memories come to mind. These memories may evoke in her a special need to be cared for and protected. As part of this psychological regression a mother needs to feel safe, to be held, and to be cared for. When this need is not met, a woman may feel abandoned, lonely, and insecure. In our culture the husband's support is essential for a mother, but he too has similar needs during this period. As we saw earlier, the doula's presence makes both father and mother feel safe. The father, too, is relieved of the heavy weight of responsibility that the doula carries.

Having a baby can place an unexpected strain on a marital relationship. For couples to bear up under the fatigue, the role and work changes, and the disruption of eating, sleeping, sex, and social activities, each partner needs to make a major effort at being understanding, supportive and communicative. It is hard to imagine how very tired parents can become when their baby's feeding schedules and needs do not follow any normal day–night cycle. Taking turns with the "nighttime watch" can help, but a couple's most important step is to share feelings. Also, the father needs to show an awareness of the strain on the mother's system after giving birth, which is natural.

Couples do best if they already communicate well before the baby is born, if they have similar ideas about parenting, and if the father has truly wanted the baby. If conflicts arise, the couple can benefit from discussing these feelings and differences with an objective person, such as a counselor or other professional.

THE POSTPARTUM DOULA AND OTHER SOURCES OF SUPPORT

In a small number of communities a type of service is extending the doula concept to care for the family following birth. These services have been called home doula programs. (See Chapter 9.) (As noted in Chapter 1, the first use of the word *doula* in the United States was actually for a woman who assisted in breast-feeding.[33]) When it is financially possible, parents engage the services of such a woman, who comes into the home to support them in whatever way needed, such as light housekeeping and food preparation, and when requested, experienced tips on baby care and breast-feeding. In this system the mother and father remain the main nurturing care-takers for the baby, but with this home doula they do not have to worry about the meals, the house, or the other extra housekeeping occasioned by the baby. The mother is encouraged to rest, and some of her many emotional and physical needs are met.

For many women this function has been met over the years by their mother or mother-in-law, or another relative or friend. Parents have learned that it is important to define the role of such a helper in advance, to consider whether they have the same philosophy of child care and whether the relationship is a supportive but not overbearing one. For instance, it may be risky for a new mother to choose her mother-in-law if she cannot communicate easily with her or with her own mother if there are still unresolved conflicts. The parents need assistance and support with the new baby and any siblings, but they do not need to fight old battles. The more the mother is cared for, the more easily she can manage the baby. The more praise and support she receives, the more love and

patience she will have with the infant. Praise and understanding from the father have been shown to enhance the mother's positive feelings about her baby and herself.

A study of 186 separate, representative nonindustrialized societies throughout the world shows that in 183 of them, mothers and babies stay together for days or weeks after delivery (the equivalent of rooming-in), and virtually none are permitted either the degree of separation that was once routine in many maternity hospitals in the United States or the type of demands and pressures on the new mother that occur today.[16, 25] In most nonindustrialized societies the mother and baby are placed together, with support, protection, and isolation from other demands and peo-

The parents and doula look on as the nurse examines the baby shortly after birth.

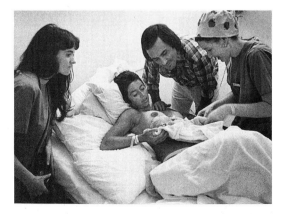

ple for at least seven days—and sometimes for weeks—after birth. In China the custom has been to have such a period for forty days. In India, new mothers are often cared for in their own mothers' homes for several weeks. The provision of food, water, warmth, and a private time for the mother and infant to get to know each other is the rule in most cultures.

In many industrialized societies in Europe, parental leave is provided, ranging from a minimum of three months to a year or more, often with full pay for part of this time and in some countries provision for the father and mother to share this leave. In addition, many services are provided for the mother and infant, for example, in England daily visits by health visitors for the first fourteen days after discharge from the hospital. These health visitors help bathe the baby, check on the condition of the mother and baby, answer questions, and arrange for additional services when special situations arise. In Holland, if a mother delivers at home, a baby nurse stays with her for ten days postpartum to help around the house. These services are made available to all mothers. In recognition of the importance of mothers and their babies, the government provides additional funds and services to all mothers during pregnancy and the period of infancy.

As we were developing our concept of the process of parent-to-infant bonding, we were attracted to the writings of the psychoanalyst D. W. (Donald) Winnicott on "primary maternal preoccupation."[39] He noted that in the perinatal period there is a special mental state of the mother in which she has a greatly increased sensitivity to and focus upon the needs of her baby. Such a state begins toward the end of the pregnancy and continues for a few weeks after the birth of the child. Mothers need support, nurturing, and a protected environment to develop and maintain this state.

"Only if a mother is sensitized in the way I am describing," wrote Winnicott, "can she feel herself into her infant's place, and so meet the infant's needs." In our own research, we have observed many examples of the special sensitivity of the mother in picking up the subtle signals of her infant, whether a fragile, tiny, premature baby or a robust, healthy, full-term one.

Using the term "holding environment," Winnicott indicated that a mother shows love to her infant through physical and emotional holding, which is crucial for the child's physical and emotional development. He felt that mothers who have the capacity to provide "good-enough care" will be helped by being supported and cared for themselves in a way that recognizes their important maternal task.

In the hectic atmosphere of a modern hospital, the heightened sensitivity of primary maternal preoccupation is sometimes misinterpreted by physicians and nurses as excessive anxiety. Once the parents are at home, the importance of this period may not be sufficiently recognized. Mothers have expectations of being perfect mothers—handling baby, work, and life as usual—and fathers need wives to be back to normal quickly, back to handling home, job, and their usual relationship. When this does not occur, a mother may feel guilty, and a father may be critical and unsympathetic.

Many women feel distressed that they cannot do everything as easily as before, or they may wonder if life will ever return to normal. Sometimes a mother in this period may question her own desire to return to work: "I'm so in love with this baby, I never want to leave him. Will I ever want to go back to work? Is something the matter with me?" Women have even told us how they have held back on becoming fully attached to their babies because they knew they would have to go back to work soon, or because they had such severe, sad, and upsetting reactions when they went back to school or work early with the previous baby

that they did not want to go through this wrenching emotional reaction again.

POSTPARTUM DEPRESSION

The "baby blues" mentioned earlier are characterized by a short period of emotional lability, commonly occurring between the second and fifth postpartum day and affecting between 80 and 90 percent of new mothers. In contrast, the term *postpartum depression* refers to a group of poorly defined, severe, depressive-type symptoms, which usually begin at four to eight weeks postpartum but, sometimes, later in the first year and which can persist for more than a year. In the past, women with these symptoms rarely sought treatment or were hospitalized. The incidence ranges from 10 to 16 percent of new mothers.[28]

The symptoms of postpartum depression cover a wide range, including exhaustion, irritability, frequent crying, feelings of helplessness and hopelessness, lack of energy and motivation so that the woman's ability to function is disturbed, lack of interest in sexual intercourse, disturbances of appetite and sleep, and feelings of being unable to cope with the new demands placed on them. Anxiety, a very frequent feature, is often related to the infant's welfare and may persist in spite of reassurance by physicians and nurses. It shows up in some mothers as lack of affection for the baby and, in turn, self-blame and guilt. Mothers may be concerned that they are not able to measure up to their own image of the ideal mother. It is not uncommon for a woman suffering from postpartum depression to have psychosomatic symptoms such as headache, backache, vaginal discharge, and abdominal pain for which no organic cause can be found.

It is important to point out that mothers working to meet the demands of their new babies and missing sleep may find that some of these symptoms fit their own situation. A mild appearance of one or more of these feelings is normal. When they are many and continue over a period of weeks, help is needed. The outlook for mothers suffering from postpartum depression is good if the diagnosis is made early and treatment is started. When there is a long delay in starting treatment, the depression may be prolonged. Often short-term psychotherapy is all that is needed. Simply having someone to talk to is very helpful in working out these symptoms.

Most studies show that a person's previous history or a family history of psychiatric problems increases the chances of postpartum depression. However, in most cases psychosocial factors are very important. The effects of unfavorable life events or chronic problems such as bereavement, unemployment, inadequate income, unsatisfactory housing, or unsupportive relations may be intensified by the fact that the new mother feels trapped and unable to change her circumstances. The experience of childbirth may bring back to her the emotional reactions related to unresolved grief for a previous stillbirth, miscarriage, or abortion, or for the death of her own mother. When a mother has had a poor relationship with her own mother or was separated from one or both parents before the age of eleven, she is more likely to be depressed and anxious, according to research. The mother's inability to confide in her partner or a friend has been noted as a factor in depression. Women are often embarrassed to tell anyone how bad they feel. Loneliness, isolation, and lack of support are serious problems for today's mothers. At the same time, mothers find it hard to reconcile the discrepancy between the hoped-for fantasy and the reality of motherhood.

Recognizing postpartum depression is important not only for the understanding and treatment of the mother, but also because of its negative effects on the relationship between the mother and the baby, and on the child's learning and social and emotional development. Preventing postpartum depression is the

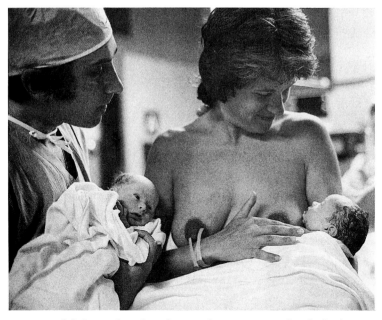

Proud father and mother of twins thirty minutes after the birth.

best way to avoid such effects, and social support is one of the most vital factors in prevention.

PROTECTING THE FAMILY IN THE FIRST WEEKS

IN THE HOSPITAL

Immediately after birth it is important that parents have private time with their baby. If the mother plans to breast-feed, she should begin to suckle or let the infant touch her nipple during this period, usually by one hour after delivery.

Reviewing the events of labor and de-livery with the doula (or nurse-midwife) is very helpful. We have found that the mother and father frequently have differ-ent ideas about what occurred and that these may differ significantly from the observations of others present. The par-ents' misconceptions are understandable, given their lack of experience with the hospital environment and their intense emotional involvement. However, they need not carry misconceptions about one another's performance or about hazards or damage to the baby when these can be clarified in the early postpartum period.

Short as the time in the hospital may be, it is extremely important for the nurses, midwives, and physicians to do their best to prepare the parents for what they will encounter when they take the baby home. First, before the mother is discharged, every effort should be made to be certain that she knows she has a normal, healthy baby (if this is the case). Initial questions about the baby's breathing or general behavior should be answered clearly and fully before discharge, or else a definite follow-up course of action (such as checking the baby's bilirubin level the day after discharge) should be planned. The hospital staff and the doula offer basic breast-feeding information. Studies have shown that the sooner after delivery mothers start breast-feeding and the more frequently they nurse their babies in the first two weeks, the more abundant their milk supply and the greater the babies' weight gain.[3] If there are any difficulties with breast-feeding, such as cracked nipples, a call to a lactation consultant or the local La Leche League will usually answer the question or problem. A recent study shows that if the mother carries the baby on her body in one of the specially made carriers, the baby will cry much less and at one year will have a more secure sense of himself or herself.[1]

AT HOME

It is most important for the parents to arrange for someone they are comfortable with to help at home after the birth. This person can be a relative or an experienced friend who shares the parents' ideas about the care and feeding of the infant and will let the parents handle the baby while the helper manages the household. Parents should plan to have someone who can nurture and support them for as long a period as possible. In addition to help from friends or relatives, there are postpartum services available, such as the home doulas mentioned earlier, nannies, or housekeepers.

If the father can arrange to take time off, he can perform many important tasks and provide much support, but the mother may wish to have the help of another woman. She may find it easier to talk with another woman about her most personal fears and anxieties, her emotional reactions—positive and negative—and any physical discomfort such as the episiotomy pain. After a cesarean delivery, a mother's needs will be intensified because her fatigue and discomfort will be greater. In all cases, the more the mother is cared for, supported, and protected, the better she will be able to care for her baby.

The father or a postpartum doula should have the responsibility for making sure the mother is not overwhelmed with too many visitors or phone calls for too long. The mother who can rest during the day, who does not feel the need to entertain with conversation and refreshments, faces the little ups and downs of her baby's course with infinitely more equanimity, adaptability, and good humor than a stressed, fatigued mother who talks on the phone for long periods and must entertain she carries the infant in a Snugli-like carrier on her body, the less the baby will cry. Studies have also shown that if the response to a baby's cry or fuss occurs within ninety seconds, the baby will quiet rapidly.[37] To get to know her

A brother explores his new sister.

guests until they go home at 11:00 P.M. Relaxation exercises continue to be useful in the postpartum period.

The more frequently the mother breast-feeds her baby in the first two or three weeks and, as we said, the more baby and get off to a good start, a mother needs plenty of time, as well as extra support, protection, and care during the first two or three months.

Parents need to take time to communicate with each other, to hear each other's feelings, and to check out how each other is doing.

Most women find it very valuable to meet with other new mothers during the first six months postpartum. It is useful to look for new mothers' groups in the local area. As during the birthing process, mothers can benefit immeasurably by sharing experiences with others who understand their feelings and appreciate their new challenges. Emotional and physical support of new parents that continues after the birth will enhance the well-being of the whole family.

9

. . .

HOW TO FIND AND
CHOOSE A DOULA

. . .

Continuous support from a doula during labor provides
physical and emotional benefits for mothers and health
bonuses for their babies. With less medical interventions,
fewer complications, and shorter hospital stays,
there may be financial savings as well.

HARVARD HEALTH LETTER
August, 1991

. . . IN THE PAST THIRTY YEARS many programs have been developed to help women through labor. Some, such as the Lamaze and Bradley methods, involve highly organized and structured techniques. These systems train women to provide labor support, and in most cases, train the father to act as a labor coach and help ease the mother's pain by guiding her through special breathing techniques. These methods are generally quite directive and structured. In contrast, the labor doula or childbirth assistant helps the mother in nondirective, naturalistic ways. The doula does not tell the mother what to do in a standardized fashion but follows the individual mother's pace. These distinctions are important, because many techniques appear to be similar to what the doula does, but in fact are very different.

PERSONALITY

The personal characteristics of each doula will, of course, vary. However, the following qualities are most beneficial with any doula:

1. A warm, loving, enthusiastic, compassionate and caring nature, coupled with maturity and responsibility

2. Tolerance for people of different ethnic groups, social statuses, levels of income, and lifestyles

3. Good health and the endurance both to stand for long periods and to work for long stretches in a crowded labor room in varied labor situations

4. The ability to deal with and remain supportive of women who may become unusually distressed during the final stages of labor

5. Experience of childbirth, either personally and also through attendance at many births

6. Comfort with touch

7. The ability to communicate, especially to listen

8. The ability to submerge her own personal belief system about maternity practices

9. The ability to be flexible and to work in a variety of birth settings with changes in staff and care providers

In addition to considering the qualities just mentioned, parents may find the following questions helpful to explore when interviewing a doula:

- What training and experience with birth does the doula have?
- What is her philosophy about supporting mothers and fathers during labor?
- Is she willing to meet with the mother and father, preferably in their home, well before labor to find out their pref

erences and hopes, and help them plan for the birth?
- Is she available to provide support and reassurance close to the time of birth and during early labor—by close phone contact and later, her presence?
- What hospitals does she work at in the parents' community?
- Does she have a backup in case she is ill?
- What are her fees?
- At what point in labor does she like to be called?
- What does she consider the most important elements of care when working as a doula?

As we mentioned earlier, the term *doula* has been applied to several different roles. In this book we have primarily described the labor-support doula or the childbirth assistant. In Chapter 8 we saw another type of doula—the postpartum doula who provides support in the home to the mother after the baby is born, helping with both the house and the baby. A third type of doula (for whom the term was first used) is a woman with broad knowledge of breast-feeding, who consults with new nursing mothers.

In some programs the term *doula* is used for volunteer women who help pregnant teenagers and other expectant mothers with special needs, such as single, unsupported women. These doulas start providing support early in pregnancy (at three months) and continue their close tie after delivery until the child is a year and a half or more. In this expanded role of the doula, each volunteer works with only one woman—meeting with her once or twice a week during the pregnancy; going with her to the prenatal clinic visits; acting as a support doula during labor, delivery, and the postpartum period; and helping with the multiple challenges and adjustments as the mother cares for her new baby. We have observed these services in Traverse City and Pontiac, Michigan, and Santa Rosa, California.

TRAINING

Most doulas have had two types of training: didactic and experiential. The didactic includes classes in the physiology of birth and the effects and techniques of giving emotional support during labor. Experiential training usually includes hands-on apprenticeship at a number of

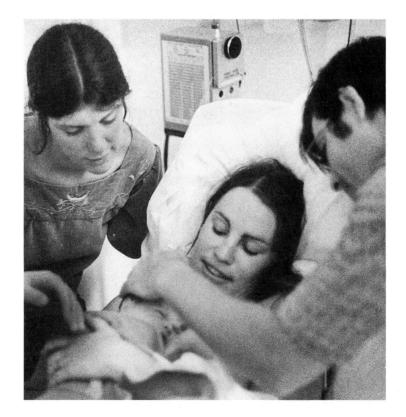

births supervised, where possible, by experienced doulas. (See the description of training in Appendix A.)

NATIONAL PROGRAMS

The oldest national certified program that trains doulas, or childbirth assistants, is the National Association of Childbirth Assistants (NACA), located in San Jose, California. (See Appendix B.) NACA not only trains women to become doulas but also teaches and certifies women who wish to create doula training programs in their own community. NACA also has a national referral system. The following is their description of the services a trained childbirth assistant offers:

> A childbirth assistant is a specially trained individual who provides skilled non-medical support for pregnancy, birth, and postpartum. She is the person who will work with you in writing your birth plan and evaluating your choices, supporting your decisions in a non-judgmental fashion, and assist you in communication skills to use with members of your birth team. During labor and birth she can reflect to you the normalcy of birth and reflect to the hospital staff your needs as an individual. She offers continuity of care throughout the birth experience and is prepared to offer the physical and emotional comfort measures you and your partner will need. During the postpartum period she can provide support and information regarding breast-feeding, transition to your new role as parents, information about newborns, and resources for community support.

LOCAL PROGRAMS

Local training programs have also evolved in various regions of the country. Among these are the following individual practices we have visited. (See Appendix B for addresses.)

The Pacific Area Labor Support (PALS) program, organized and led by Penny Simkin in Seattle, Washington, has long had an interest in childbirth support and is an excellent model training program and service unit for doulas. Twice a year, a four-day course is given on two weekends. After this didactic course, the women complete an apprenticeship and expand their skills by observing and assisting an experienced doula before starting out on their own. Once trained, doulas may be certified by the organization and placed on the PALS referral list. The training continues with ongoing group meetings of the doulas—a key element—so they can continue skill-building support, share experiences, and supervise doulas-in-training.

These are extremely important elements in all of the training groups. PALS also coordinates the services for expectant mothers who need doulas in the Seattle area, as well as in Oregon, British Columbia, and other parts of Washington. Needy mothers do not pay a fee, and other women pay on a sliding-fee scale. The local public health department now subcontracts with PALS for labor-support services, and the doulas now receive a small stipend for their assistance. Similar groups with local variations include the Doula Association of Greater Cleveland and the Sonoma County Doula Project in Sebastopol, California.

Recognizing the value of this type of continuous support, obstetricians have begun to organize doulas for their patients. A model for this, called Labor Support Services and located in San Geronimo, California, uses Marin General Hospital for deliveries. Also affiliated with a hospital is the Childbirth Education Association of Jacksonville, Florida, which trains doulas who are official hospital volunteers at University Medical Center. They either go to the hospital and work with whoever needs support, or they are called by the nursing staff when a particularly needy woman arrives. These doulas also provide labor support for women who are temporarily housed in a local maternity home, for the wives or partners of naval personnel who are away on active duty, and for pregnant naval personnel who are single or unaccompanied. North Central Bronx Hospital in New York City provides volunteer doulas, who attend 5 percent of the hospital's births. Doulas work with certified nurse-midwives, who deliver most of the babies. Other hospitals have volunteer groups that provide on-call doula services for needy or unsupported women.

Many HMOs and health insurance plans are beginning to see the medical and financial value of doula support. For instance, the Rhode Island Group Health Association and Harvard Community Health Care in Massachusetts both contract with private doula services to provide referrals to mothers in their plans.

A model for private doula service is Nadia Stein in Houston, Texas, who has offered doula services for several years. She was a trainer of other doulas and is now an independent practitioner in private practice. As a doula, she has assisted in more than 150 deliveries. We have had an opportunity to observe her supportive efforts for a large number of mothers in labor and have been most impressed by her unique abilities to meet each mother's individual needs. Best Birth, based in Chicago, provides referrals, training, and certification throughout the Chicago area. These offer labor support as well as postpartum care. The Birth and Bonding International in Berkeley, California, provides care and support for women, couples, and families through classes, workshops, and doula support. A doula certification training program was initiated there in 1990.

THE SPREAD OF DOULA SERVICES

To find a labor doula in any community, we suggest beginning with the programs or doulas listed in Appendix B. If no one is listed in your community, the next step is to check with the National Association of Childbirth Assistants (NACA) or with Doulas of North America (DONA) (see Appendix B for addresses). DONA is a new international umbrella organization whose purposes are to provide certification of qualified doulas with a variety of backgrounds and experiences, establish standards of safe, responsible labor-support care; promote and publicize the concept of labor support to both the medical profession and the public; and provide communication and continuing education for doulas. If there are no doulas in your area listed with NACA or DONA, you can contact local childbirth education instructors, midwives, physicians, and hospitals for names of services or individuals offering childbirth support. (See also the addresses for the International Childbirth Education Association

and, for postpartum support, the National Association of Postpartum Care Services in Appendix B.)

The concept of doulas is new in many parts of the country but is spreading through the efforts of interested laypeople and professionals. Other innovations supportive to childbirth with which we have been involved (such as rooming-in with the newborn) have been introduced by groups of parents who, working with childbirth educators and interested nurses and doctors, have convinced local medical caregivers and administrators to try the new services. Such cooperative efforts often prove effective in bringing a change in practices. The references in the Bibliography to specific studies are useful in discussions with medical personnel.

If no other resources are available, parents may find a caring female friend or relative who has some experience with childbirth and is willing and interested in being a support person for the expectant mother and father. With the help of this book, participation in childbirth classes, and contact with experienced doulas in other areas (see Appendix B), such a woman could offer important help.

As parents begin to recognize the contribution of doula support in childbirth, and as scientific studies of such support become known, different systems of doula service based on the resources of

each specific community will evolve. The doula role varies widely, but whenever and wherever this service develops, the goal should be the same: continuous, skilled, empathetic, nonmedical emotional support of a doula to a mother and father.

We hope that some women reading this book might become interested in providing this service for other women and undertake formal training. The energy for being a doula comes from the satisfaction and joy of helping other women during childbirth. On one occasion in Cleveland, when a call went out to start a program, more than 100 women volunteered to become doulas. Having observed, assisted with, or attended many hundreds of births between us, the authors can say that no experience can possibly compare with witnessing the birth of a new human being.

APPENDIX A

. . .

THE TRAINING OF A DOULA

CHOOSING TO BECOME A DOULA

Women who have the interest and develop the special skills to become a doula may come from a variety of backgrounds, but they share a single goal: to help other women through the major life event of giving birth. Some doulas are childbirth educators who like to continue assisting couples through birth Some combine both childbirth education and labor support and also offer training to other women. Some doulas come from the home-birth or lay-midwifery movement. Some women seem to have a natural bent for the whole birth process, just as some people are born with perfect pitch, and they seek a role in which to express this talent.

Many women who choose to be doulas had support when they themselves gave birth and are so grateful for the kind of support they received that they want to "give something back." Some feel that the support they received during labor and delivery was unique and invaluable—more special than any other support they have ever received.

Other women who want to become doulas express a desire to give this kind of support because they did not receive emotional support at their own childbirth, and they realize how isolated and frightened they felt and how much they would have benefited from that support. Still other women, regardless of whether they have been previously interested or involved in birth or whether they had support during the birth of their own children, are drawn to helping other women after experiencing childbirth themselves.

Whatever the impetus or motivation to become a doula, it is essential for the doula to have a period of training and/or apprenticeship. (For addresses of training programs, see Appendix B.)

THE NATURE OF DOULA SUPPORT

Perhaps the most important insight needed by a doula-in-training is that every woman comes to labor with a different set of life experiences, needs, coping mechanisms, and responses. Each comes with a particular set of birth stories, information, worries, and histories. She approaches birth with her individual expectations and varied abilities to deal with pain or other difficult situations. The father, partner, close relative, or friend who accompanies the mother also comes with past life experiences and concerns. For this reason the doula must be adaptable, resourceful, and often creative to meet the different needs of each woman and the person accompanying her at birth.

Doula support is, by definition, personalized. Through a dynamic interaction with the mother and father (or other partner) the doula adjusts her care to the individual mother's needs. For this reason, doula training must be designed both to specify minimum support standards and to provide the trainees with a wide variety of techniques to use as required. In addition, basic information about hospital procedures and about labor and delivery is clearly important.

The doula's communication to the laboring woman occurs at a visceral level. She breathes with the woman; she feels with the woman; she tends to the emotions of the woman. Medical caregivers often communicate only at an intellectual level. They are responsible for medical outcomes and must monitor for possible risks and be familiar with the technology available for complicated births. Both roles, of course, are important.

BASIC TRAINING

The content and scheduling of training programs vary, but each contains both courses and actual experience. Courses include discussions and introduction to the basic physiological, psychological, and emotional changes during pregnancy, labor, delivery, and the early postpartum period. Discussions also include descriptions of the layout of the labor and delivery area and, if possible, introductions to the medical and nursing staff of the local hospital. The training will include experiential exercises in communication skills, empathy training, and ways to create comfort through touch and words, as well as role-playing of common situations and ways to empower women. Literature for the training will vary, but we urge all trainees to read the basic medical studies that support the beneficial effects of the doula. (See Chapter 3 and Simkin,[35] Perez,[32] Kitzinger,[18] and Odent[30] in particular in the References at the back of this book.)

Before beginning their clinical experience, trainees have found it very helpful to view a thirty-minute videotape that illustrates many of the actual techniques of labor support with experienced doulas. After the first few lectures, it is useful for the doula trainees to observe an experienced doula during an actual labor and birth. The lectures then become more alive, and the trainers can refer to events that the trainees have observed.

Training sessions should allow trainees to experience a variety of supportive techniques used by doulas; the mothers' varied responses to the support; interactions between the doulas, the fathers, and the medical staff; and changes in support when necessary as labor progresses. After observing or assisting with a birth, trainees should have a chance to discuss not only alternative techniques in a given situation but also their feelings about each technique and about the laboring woman's behavior. In this way they can develop confidence and comfort in their own abilities to become doulas. We believe that most of the training should center around hands-on experience and the development of communication and counseling skills. After the initial training and for their first solo, doulas may gain much by discussing each case in detail with another doula (if possible, within a day or two after the birth). This type of continuing dialogue will remain useful over an entire career. Periodic small-group discussions with three to six doulas have proven especially helpful. Doulas, whether volunteer or paid, will benefit from and appreciate ongoing skill development, continued training, and interpersonal support.

*GENERAL GUIDELINES**

- A doula helps and encourages a mother to deal with labor *as best she can.* There is no right or wrong way for her to do this, and no ideal against which she is being measured. Take time to assess how the mother is working with her labor, and then build on it. Help her call on her inner strength to deal with labor; help her help herself. Demonstrate your confidence—through your words and facial expressions—that she *can* cope with labor and birth.

- Encourage, praise, and reassure the mother. When labor is intense, she may need constant reminders that she is feeling and experiencing the normal sensations of labor, not something to fear. Tell her what a terrific job she's doing! Remind her that she is managing and that she will continue to be able to cope with each contraction as it comes.

- Help the mother stay focused on the present (not on how long it has been or how long it will be). Help her deal only with the pain of the moment. The experience in a given moment is

rarely so intense that it can not be accepted.

- It may help the mother and her partner if you describe what is happening inside her as she has contractions. Create an image for her to focus on. Some laboring women find it very effective to close their eyes and visualize what they want to have happen in their labor (the cervix opening, contractions getting stronger, the baby moving down).

- Be ready at all times with a touch, words, or a look. If the mother gets lost or overwhelmed during a difficult contraction, tell her to blow out and breathe with you. Establish both eye and physical contact (while facing her, hold her right hand and her left shoulder, for instance). Tell her she can get through this and you will help her. You may need to be firm and directive. Use massage, touch relaxation, and stroking to encourage any tense body parts to relax during and between contractions.

- Between contractions, ask the mother what she liked or did not like. As labor progresses, keep communication simple and watch for her nonverbal cues. Don't take offense if the mother is less than polite during the intense portions of her labor. To labor effectively, she must be able to let go of the many inhibitions that rule behavior in everyday life.

*The rest of this appendix was adapted from the collected guidelines for labor companions of an experienced and sensitive certified nurse-midwife, Susan Rose, who spent many years working as a doula and training doulas. She is now a busy midwife in Hanson, Massachusetts.

- Acknowledge pain when it exists. This is essential. If the mother shows you or tells you she is hurting, acknowledge her feelings. You might respond with, "Your uterus is working very well and hard," or, "That was a good strong contraction," or, "Your baby is pressing down just the way she should be." This is pain with a purpose. Remind the mother that what she's feeling (such as pressure, pain, or stretching) is normal for labor. Remind her of what the feelings represent (for example, the cervix opening, the baby moving down).
- As labor progresses, what feels good and what is needed will change. Sometimes nothing feels good. At these times in a labor or birth, you need to help the mother accept the way she feels, keep it in perspective, relax more, and be open.
- Give the mother your total, undivided attention. Your emotional support can take the place of drugs for pain relief. Minimize distractions during the more intense parts of labor. Try to be aware of any people or things that may be upsetting the mother, and deal with them for her. Better still, support the mother in dealing with them in an appropriate manner—another facet of empowerment.
- Try to stay calm and relaxed. Your tension and anxiety are easily communicated. Deal with your fears and concerns before labor begins so that you are free to focus on the mother during labor. If you feel yourself tensing up, take a slow, deep breath and relax, or take a short break from labor, asking the father to stand in and saying when you will be back.
- Don't feel out of place or intimidated by the hospital setting, the staff, or the equipment. You are essential to the mother's well-being. Be sure to ask questions and get the information you need to feel at ease. At the same time, don't give medical advice or interfere with the medical staff's care in any way. Labor is not a time to attempt to change the practices of a maternity unit. Doulas must submerge their own beliefs about hospital practices during a birth. Be diplomatic with hospital personnel. (You are working in their territory.) Encourage the father and mother to communicate their own needs to the hospital staff.
- Focus on the mother's and father's needs, not your own. Mothers' needs come first, but many fathers also need your support and encouragement. Be sensitive to any relatives or friends who are present. Always maintain a positive attitude and model supportive behavior for the partner to use. Encourage the father to be close to and supportive of the mother at his com-

fort level. Add praise whenever possible.

- Adjust your support to each mother's needs, and alter your care to her changing requirements as she progresses through pregnancy, birth, and the postpartum period. Concentrate on relaxing and reassuring the mother without teaching specific childbirth techniques, since we do not know which procedures work best for any given woman.

EARLY FIRST STAGE OF CHILDBIRTH

The efforts of the doula or childbirth assistant during the first stage (when the cervix thins and opens) should be geared toward helping the mother have a relaxed body and a mind at peace. This allows the mother's contracting uterus to open her cervix while she conserves her energy for pushing. You can help her with the following measures.

- Have the mother stay home as long as possible. Options for comfort are much greater at home. Going into the hospital will not make things happen faster, and labor may even slow down in a strange environment. (See "Knowing When to Go into the Hospital or Birth Center," later in this appendix.)
- During this early time in labor a woman can gradually get used to the feeling of contractions. Later, as contractions become more intense, they will hurt. This pain is a normal part of the birthing process. Remind the mother that there is a purpose for the pain: it is a sign of the work her body is doing to thin and open her cervix. To help her accept and cope with the pain, you can remind her that she is not in this alone.
- It is essential for a woman to take nourishment in the form of fluids or easily digestible proteins and carbohydrates. A dehydrated or starved body cannot labor as effectively as a well-nourished one. Also, the baby continues to be totally dependent on her for nourishment throughout labor. Suggest that she eat a good meal early in labor, and have her continue to drink plenty of liquids and avoid high-fat foods and concentrated sweets (candy). The mother might wish to try juice, fruit, yogurt, whole-wheat bread or crackers, nourishing soup, and other foods that appeal to her. As labor progresses, she may not feel like eating, but encourage her to *drink.* Labor is hard work, and she will need lots of fluid to meet her body's needs. If fruit juices (or fruit-juice Popsicles) do not appeal to her, suggest noncaffeinated soft drinks, which will give her the energy she needs without making her feel jittery. Nausea is normal for some

women in labor and is not the result of drinking or eating.

- Suggest a warm bath (if the membranes are intact) to help her stay more comfortable and relaxed. Fill the tub as high as possible. Have her kneel in the tub or lie back against pillows. Put the pillows in a garbage sack with a towel over the plastic to keep them dry. Keep a comfortably hot, wet towel over her belly and groin during contractions. She might want a cool drink and a cool cloth for her head. Be sure to give this a try, especially at times in labor when the mother feels that nothing will help.

  If the woman's membranes have ruptured, suggest that she try a shower. Put a chair in so that she can sit or lean on it. If she does not feel like bathing or showering or if a bathtub or shower is not available, apply warm, wet towels to her abdomen, groin, or back.

- Have the mother *walk*. Walking tends to shorten labor, reduce the need for pain-relieving drugs, decrease fetal heart-rate abnormalities, and improve the baby's condition during labor and birth. A doula and other support people may need to keep encouraging the mother (strongly!) to walk.

- Women in labor should change positions often—at least every thirty to sixty minutes. This can help to avoid or correct fetal distress, as well as speed labor. Positions such as standing, squatting, and kneeling while leaning forward are excellent. They can increase uterine activity, shorten labor by helping the cervix dilate more efficiently, and reduce discomfort. Other good positions for labor include sitting, lying on the side, and being up on the hands and knees. Use lots of pillows to help the mother feel comfortable. She should *not* lie flat on her back because this can cause a drop in her blood pressure and a decreased blood flow (and therefore decreased oxygen) to her baby.

- Laboring women should urinate every hour. A full bladder can inhibit uterine activity and be an obstacle to the baby's birth. If a woman is having trouble urinating during labor, try having her listen to the sound of running water, pour warm water over her vaginal area while she sits on the toilet, or have her relax on the toilet with her hand in a bowl of warm water.

LATE FIRST STAGE OF CHILDBIRTH

During the late first stage of labor, most women strongly need other people (their support people) to help them cope with and accept the intense contractions that are normal for this time in labor. Labor is truly easier when a woman has people to encourage and reassure her during this time. If she is going to a hospital or birth center for her baby's birth, the best time to make the trip is usually late in the first stage. Whether at home or in the hospital or birth center, the following measures will continue to be helpful.

- Have the mother continue with warm baths or showers, hot towels, position changes, walking, nourishment, and frequent urination. Try other comfort measures such as cold compresses, pressure on the back, pelvic rocking, massages or stroking. Let the mother use extra pillows, a bean bag, or you or the father to lean against for added comfort. What feels good often changes as labor progresses, so remember to try again with comfort measures that may not have been helpful earlier.
- This is an intense time. The mother may need to maintain contact with you through every contraction. You can talk and breathe her through contractions, use a loving touch, and maintain eye contact. Then help her rest, relax, and refresh herself between contractions. Visualizations and imagery are also extremely useful to help the mother work through the contractions.
- Ask the mother to show or tell you not only how and where to touch her but also what feels good and what does not.

- Help the mother stay upright and walking as long as possible. Alternate periods of activity and rest as needed. She may need a lot of encouragement to change positions, walk, or urinate. Remember, these activities will help her labor progress normally.
- Many women experience a time in labor when they are in a lot of pain and cannot get comfortable. If the mother experiences these feelings, help her concentrate on releasing tension and yielding to the intense contractions. Emotional support and focus on relaxation (in spite of the intensity of the contractions) will get her through this difficult time. Reassure her that she *can* do it. Have her deal with her contractions *one at a time* and not think about how long it has been or how long it will be.

KNOWING WHEN TO GO INTO THE BIRTH CENTER OR HOSPITAL

Experience with previous births and close contact with the midwife or physician enables you, the doula, to help the mother interpret what she is feeling and what is happening during her labor.

In deciding when to have the mother go to the hospital, be sure to consider what the weather is like, how far the mother is from the hospital or birth center, whether this is a first baby (labor and birth are often longer than with subsequent babies), and how strongly the mother feels about being settled in at the place where the baby will be born.

Several signs can help you and the mother decide when to leave home to go to the birth center or hospital. For most women these signs tend to be present in the late first stage, but every woman is different. The mother may experience none of these signs or one or more of them:

- The mother's face may become deeply flushed (red). This flushing, which looks like what some women experience after orgasm, may extend to her upper chest. This sign alone does not mean it is urgent to get to the hospital.
- The mother may have an increase of bloody, mucousy show. Again, there is usually no rush, and you might wait for other signs to develop. (This is not heavy, bright red bleeding with blood running down her leg. Have her consult with the doctor or midwife if she has constant bleeding or any questions or concerns about the bloody show she is experiencing.)
- Long, strong contractions with little rest in between, combined with shaking legs or arms, nausea or vomiting, or hiccups are typical late-first-stage signs. If these appear, consider going to the hospital.
- After a period of long, strong, close contractions (usually with increased

bloody show and a deep flush on the face), a woman may experience a lull in labor, with contractions slowing down and easing up. This may be the normal resting point or plateau many women seem to experience after becoming completely dilated and before an urge to push develops. Help the mother enjoy the rest, and go to the birthing location. Be aware that there are other plateau points in labor. Some women experience plateaus at around three or four centimeters of dilatation and/or around seven or eight centimeters.

- She may find herself pushing or feeling an urge to push with contractions. She may feel increasing rectal pressure (as though she needs to have a bowel movement) during or between contractions. If so, have her breathe or blow through these contractions, and go straight to the hospital.
- A mother may feel she needs to go to the birthing location. Sometimes she may feel or sense something that you do not see. If she wants to go to the birthing location even though she may still be in early first stage and you are not able to help her feel more at ease or comfortable at home, she should go in. If she is in early labor (less than four centimeters dilatation) and everything is fine after she is checked, consider going back home (if she is close by) or for a walk in the building or

neighborhood until labor has progressed further.

Moving out of the familiar surroundings of home into the unfamiliarity of the hospital can create feelings of anxiety and fear. These feelings heighten the perception of pain, and they can help elevate stress hormones (adrenalin and noradrenalin), which may slow or stop contractions. It is common to hear reports of labors progressing well at home but stalling when the mother arrives at the hospital. Animal studies have shown that when animal mothers are frightened, labor stops. This may represent nature's way to let the laboring female flee a potential danger. Fear may be reduced by the sense of trust and empowerment a woman develops during pregnancy while working with a doula.

Some couples who are familiar with the hospital's practices because of childbirth classes or former positive birth experiences may arrive with confidence that the experts will take over and relieve the mother's discomfort or pain. However, almost all women arrive at the hospital with a vulnerability peculiar to the state of childbirth—the unconscious feelings of fear, anxiety, and insecurity about the unknown. Many women associate hospitals with illness and the role of a patient, as well as with a

potential for danger, use of unexpected procedures, a lack of privacy, isolation, and confusion about high-tech equipment. There may also be rules that prohibit a woman from following her own instinctive body positions such as walking or crouching. Women in labor are particularly sensitive to harsh or brusque words or an impersonal tone of voice from busy, harassed, or tired personnel.

The most important factor in alleviating the anxiety that most women feel upon arrival at the hospital is the attitude of the people helping her. The presence of a doula makes a difference here. Having already established a relationship with the mother in advance, a doula gives the mother the confidence and security of knowing there is one person who will remain and be committed to her. The calming presence of the doula, combined with the mother's own sense of confidence achieved by prenatal preparation, can keep her focused on her labor, continuing to relax through contractions even in the car, at triage or admitting, and through the often disruptive activities, interventions, and general busyness typical of a hospital.

THE HOSPITAL-BASED DOULA

If support is given by a hospital-based labor doula called on to assist a newly arrived woman who is accompanied or unaccompanied by another person, she will have to start creating that calm and comforting presence as soon as she is introduced. She can put her hand on the mother's hand or arm and let the mother know that she will be with her throughout her labor. Whenever the doula first meets the mother, her role remains constant: creating a continuous presence and offering reassurance, touch, verbal and nonverbal comfort, relaxation, and praise.

If the woman has never met a doula and seems frightened, the hospital-based doula may address the fear, asking the mother if she is afraid, acknowledging that the mother may have heard all kinds of scary stories, and responding quietly but confidently. The doula then explains what is happening in the woman's body, how normal and natural it is, and how capable her body is of having a baby. She can begin to encourage the mother to trust her body, to let it do what it wants to do, to not be afraid, to let the fear go, and to not fight against her body. She teaches the mother to breathe through the contractions and lets her know that she will help her. A frightened mother will often look at the doula and begin to feel much calmer and will start to relax. Reducing a mother's fear and anxiety lessens her stress responses, which include the secretion of adrenalin.[23,24] Since adrenalin decreases

uterine contractions and lengthens labor, any reduction of fears and anxiety by the doula will permit labor to progress more normally.

In this first encounter a doula may repeat words similar to those used by Nadia Stein, an experienced doula mentioned in Chapter 9: "Nothing to be scared about—birth is normal and natural and your body knows what to do. Remember, let your body go through, let it go through, just breathe it through freely, quietly, letting go. Relax as much as you can; just breathe it through. That's it, you see—that's just the only thing you have to do; that will help you through." A doula can repeat this same pattern of words quietly, in a rhythm, three or four times. Nadia noted: "As the woman is gaining control, the fear begins to leave. This whole sequence may take only five or ten minutes through two or three contractions—the mother begins to understand what you mean, and she knows you are helping her and that it becomes easier. So even a frightened woman begins to gain confidence in what she is doing, and even knowing that it is painful, she feels she can stand it and she understands how much being relaxed helps her."

This initial contact and the mother's initial sense of letting go and being in control of her own labor (in the sense of not being panicked) become powerful unconscious foundations for the rest of labor. As the doula continues to stay, maintaining physical contact and using a comforting voice, these important elements get reinforced.

THE SECOND STAGE OF CHILDBIRTH

The doula's efforts and those of the father during the second stage (when the cervix is completely open and the mother pushes her baby out) should be geared not only toward helping her cooperate with her body but also toward providing a calm, peaceful atmosphere into which her new child will be born.

During this stage you, the doula, can help in the following ways:

· There is nothing magical about a woman being at ten centimeters, or completely dilated. Some women feel an urge to push before ten centimeters, and others feel it considerably after this point.

· If the mother does not feel an urge to push, try getting her into a gravity-assisted (upright) position and continue to breathe with her through contractions. Walking, squatting, or sitting on the toilet often helps at this time. Remind the mother to be patient, relax, and wait for a pushing urge to develop as her baby moves farther down her birth canal. Waiting until the urge to push develops allows her to coordinate her pushing efforts with those of her uterus. If her physician or midwife feels it is necessary to birth her baby quickly, she or he will direct her on how and when to push.

· Have the woman urinate before she begins pushing.

· Any positions used for labor can also be used for pushing and for the baby's birth. Each position has advantages and disadvantages. A mother who has practiced during pregnancy and experimented during labor may know the most comfortable and effective position(s). Help her change positions at least every half hour if she has a long or difficult second stage. Upright positions that use gravity may be helpful. Squatting uses gravity and allows maximum opening of the pelvic outlet. Standing sometimes helps if the baby is still high in the pelvis. Sitting on the toilet is excellent for opening up and releasing the whole pelvic area. Lying on one side can be helpful in slowing a quick descent, but less helpful if the baby is coming slowly. Upright positions can aggravate hemorrhoids; lying on the side does not. All-fours positions do not use gravity, but they do take pressure off the back and allow spreading of the hips and pelvic bones. Both all-fours and squatting positions are good for a large or posterior baby. The doctor or midwife may suggest different positions for the mother to try while pushing.

- Avoid letting the mother lie flat on her back. If she is semireclining, you or the father can sit behind her to prop her up, or you can use pillows or raise the head of the birthing bed or delivery table so that she is not lying flat.

- The mother will need frequent assurance that the intense and painful sensations she may feel—backache, nausea, hot flashes, trembling legs, spreading sensations in the pelvis, intense pressure on the rectum, an urge to empty the bowels, involuntary bearing down, intense pressure as the baby descends through the birth canal, or burning and stretching sensations as the vaginal outlet opens to accommodate her baby—are normal and that she *can* stretch and open enough to give birth to her baby.

- Remind her to work with her body— let her body tell her what to do to get her baby out. She can bear down (push) when, how, and however long her body demands that. Encourage her to ease up on pushing if it hurts or if burning sensations occur. She may want to see and touch her baby's head as it emerges from her body. This contact may renew her spirits and energy, and help her focus on bringing her baby out.

- When pushing, she might at times breathe out, make noise, or hold her breath. Many women have found that certain kinds of noises like grunts and moaning sounds help them give birth to their babies. Help her not to be inhibited about making sounds—that is a natural part of the birthing process for many women, and she will find what works for her if she goes ahead and tries it. Many women find that releasing sound opens the throat and subsequently the birth canal. Whatever works for her is fine. However, have her avoid prolonged breath holding.

- During a long second stage, a woman needs nourishment to keep up or restore her energy level. Spoonfuls of honey (or drinks sweetened with honey) or juice will provide a quick source of energy.

- You can encourage her to release and open for the birth. If you watch her mouth, shoulders, and legs for signs of tension, you can help her release these areas.

- She may be so intently focused on the work of giving birth that she does not hear what others are saying. You can help by keeping the mother informed of what is happening and conveying instructions from the doctor or midwife.

- Try to keep the atmosphere calm and peaceful, so that the mother and father can enjoy the birth (and the end of labor) and especially the new life they have brought forth.

Even when a labor does not proceed as planned, the doula still plays an important role. For example, if oxytocin is administered, contractions sometimes become more intense and painful. This is a time to help the mother relax even more, by leading her in breathing through the contractions or by engaging her in more deepening relaxation visualizations.

If there is a possibility of a problem and the mother requires constant fetal monitoring or more than the usual monitoring, further calming of the mother may reduce the problem and will certainly reassure her.

If there is a cesarean section, the doula will need to reassure the parents that she will remain with them. Also, she will need to remain positive and make sure that the parents understand step-by-step what is going to take place. The doula can also help a mother realize that having a cesarean section is not her failure.

When a mother is given an epidural, it is important to give her gentle encouragement to make the birth hers. A doula can remind the mother, "Your baby is getting everything it needs. What a great mom you are going to be. You know exactly what's right for your baby. You're doing just fine." Both the common as well as the uncommon situations that can arise during labor should be discussed during training.

Many doulas find it useful with each delivery to keep a record that includes the length of labor, the place of birth (at home or in the hospital), the delivery outcome (vaginal or cesarean section), the use of any drugs, the use of forceps, and any complications for the mother or the infant. A short questionnaire for parents has provided useful feedback for doulas in evaluating the effect of their services. Questions can include the following: Was having a doula helpful to you and your partner? What aspects of support helped? What aspects of support were not useful? What changes or additions of support would you make? Would you use a doula again? Do you have any other suggestions or comments?

Though the work can be exhausting, there are unusual rewards. Doulas describe a barrage of powerful and positive emotions after a birth. They describe a unique euphoria that often lasts up to twelve hours. They feel good in a way they have not previously sensed. They cannot just walk out the door. The images keep coming for a long time afterward. They and the families share a sense of warmth and connectedness. Being part of such an intense, intimate, and critical experience has been very satisfying and valuable for all the doulas we have known. One doula said: "It's hard to believe how close we become. It's the most important thing I do. After I go home, I feel close to my children. I relive my own childbirth experience. I want to talk to another doula. I need to talk to someone, to debrief, to share how it was."

APPENDIX B

. . .

USEFUL ADDRESSES

FOR INFORMATION ON DOULAS,
LABOR SUPPORT, AND REFERRALS:

Doulas of North America (DONA)
1100 23rd Avenue E.
Seattle, WA 98112
Fax: (206) 325-0472

National Association of Childbirth
   Assistants (NACA)
205 Copco Lane
San Jose, CA 95123
(408) 225-9167

International Association of Parents
   and Professionals for Safe
   Alternatives in Childbirth
   (NAPSAC)
Route 1, Box 646
Marble Hill, MO 63764
(314) 238-2010

American College of Nurse Midwives
   (ACNM)
1522 K Street NW, Suite 1000
Washington, DC 20005
(202) 289-0171

Association of Birth Assistants (ABA)
60 Fern Valley Crest
Richmond Hill
Ontario L4E 2J1
Canada
(416) 773-4069

*REGIONAL DOULA REFERRALS AND
SERVICES:*

This list is incomplete and subject to
change as new services are formed
around the country. Readers are urged
to check with DONA and NACA, and
ABA in Canada, for a current list of services (see addresses above). The authors
have not had personal experience with
all of these groups.

CALIFORNIA
Birth and Bonding International
1172 San Pablo Avenue, Suite 101
Berkeley, CA 94702
(510) 527-2121

Birth Care
North San Francisco Bay Area
P.O. Box 426
El Verano, CA 95433
(707) 996-5729

The Fourth Trimester
3665A 19th Street
San Francisco, CA 94110
(415) 821-7068

Labor Support Services
P.O. Box 220
San Geronimo, CA 94963
(415) 461-7800

Mother Care
1753 King Street
Santa Cruz, CA 95060
(408) 423-3312

Sonoma County Doula Project
446 Petaluma Avenue
Sebastopol, CA 95472
(707) 823-2738

FLORIDA
Birth Companions
105 Rockledge Drive
Rockledge, FL 37955

Childbirth Education Association
8808 Arlington Expressway
Jacksonville, FL 32211
(904) 724-6696

ILLINOIS
Best Birth
2668 Hillside Lane
Evanston, IL 60201

MASSACHUSETTS
Boston Association for Childbirth
  Education
69 Court Street
Newton, MA 02160
(617) 244-5102

NEW JERSEY

From Our Hands to Yours
14 Hancock Court
Flemington, NJ 08822
(908) 806-7719

MotherLove, Inc.
20 W. Ridgewood Avenue
Ridgewood, NJ 07450

NEW YORK

MotherLove, Inc.
70 West 93rd Street #20G
New York, NY 10025
(212) 749-6613

MotherLove, Inc.
22 Tanglewood Drive
Staten Island, NY
(718) 948-8042

North Central Bronx Hospital
3424 Kossuth Avenue
Bronx, NY 10467
(718) 519-5000

Woman to Woman
4991 Route 209
Accord, NY 12404

OHIO

Doula Service of Greater Cleveland
P.O. Box 33174
Cleveland, OH 44133
(216) 237-3561
(216) 656-1763

TEXAS

Childbirth and Family Education, Inc.
415 Bauxhall Court
Katy, TX 77450
(713) 497-8894

Labor Companions
P.O. Box 11447
Fort Worth, TX 96110
(847) 924-8819

Nadia Stein
Doula Services
7110 Tickner
Houston, TX 77055
(713) 686-4658

WASHINGTON

Pacific Association for Labor Support (PALS)
1100 23rd Avenue East
Seattle, WA 98112
Fax: (206) 325-0472

MotherCare
P.O. Box 1012
Edmonds, WA 98020
(206) 771-4577

WISCONSIN

Alternative Birth Services
109 Everglade Drive
Madison, WI 53717
(608) 833-2959

International Childbirth Education
   Association (ICEA)
P.O. Box 20048
Minneapolis, MN 55420
(612) 854-8660

IH/IBP
P.O. Box 3675
Ann Arbor, MI 48106
(313) 662-6857

American College of Obstetricians and
   Gynecologists (ACOG)
409 12th Street SW
Washington, DC 20024
(202) 638-5577

INFORMATION ON BREAST-FEEDING:

La Leche League International, Inc.
P.O. Box 1209
9616 Minneapolis Avenue
Franklin Park, IL 60131
(312) 455-7730

International Lactation Consultant
   Association
P.O. Box 4031
University of Virginia Station
Charlottesville, VA 22903
(404) 381-5127

*INFORMATION ON POST-PARTUM
SUPPORT:*

National Association of Postpartum
   Care Services (NAPCS)
8910 299th Place SW
Edmonds, WA 98026

PUBLICATIONS:

Birth and Life Bookstore, Inc.
P.O. Box 70625
Seattle, WA 98107
(206) 789-4444

Mail order catalog of publications on
all aspects of childbirth and childcare

Birth
Blackwell Scientific Publications
238 Main Street
Cambridge, MA 02142
(617) 876-7000

Quarterly journal for childbirth
professionals and parents

Bookmarks
(published by ICEA—see above)

The Doula
P.O. Box 71
Santa Cruz, CA 95063
(408) 464-9488

Maternity Center
   Association/Publications
48 E. 92nd Street
New York, NY 10128
(212) 369-7300

Catalog of publications available by
mail order

Mothering
P.O. Box 1690
Santa Fe, NM 87504
(505) 984-8116

Quarterly magazine for parents

. . .

REFERENCES

1. Anisfeld, E., Casper, V.; Nozyce, M.; Cunningham, N. "Does Infant Carrying Promote Attachment? An Experimental Study of the Effects of Increased Physical Contact on the Development of Attachment." *Child Development* 61(1990): 1617–1627.

2. Bertsch, T.D.; Nagashima-Whalen, L.; Dykeman, S.; Kennell, J.H.; McGrath, S.K. "Labor Support by First-time Fathers: Direct Observations." *Journal of Psychosomatic Obstetrics and Gynecology* 11(1990):251–260.

3. DeCarvalho, M.; Robertson, S.; Friedman, A.; Klaus, M. "Effect of Frequent Breast-feeding on Early Milk Production and Infant Weight Gain." *Pediatrics* 72(1983):307–311.

4. de Regt, R.H.; Minkoff, H.L.; Feldman, J.; Schwarz, R.H. "Relation of Private or Clinic Care to the Cesarean Birth Rate." *New England Journal of Medicine* 315(1986):619–624.

5. Donnison, J. *Midwives and Medical Men: A History of the Struggle for the Control of Childbirth.* London: Heinemann, 1990.

6. Fusi, L.; Maresh, J.J.A.; Steer, P.J.; Beard, R.W. "Maternal Pyrexia Associated with the Use of Epidural Analgesia in Labor." *Lancet* 1(1989):1250–1252.

7. Halpin, G.J.; Rose, E.; Shapiro, E. "Trends in Cesarean Section Rates." *New England Journal of Medicine* 86(1989):867–873.

8. Hemminnki, E.; Virta, A.L.; Kopinen, P.; Malin, M.; Kojo-Austin, H.; Tuijmala, R. "A Trial on Continuous Human Support during Labor: Feasibility, Interventions and Mothers' Satisfaction." *Journal of Psychosomatic Obstetrics and Gynecology* (1990): 239–250.

9. Henneborn, W.J., and Cogan, R. "The Effect of Husband Participation on Reported Pain and Probability of Medication during Labour and Birth." *Journal of Psychosomatic Research* 19(1975):215–222.

10. Hodnett, E.D., and Abel, S.M. "Person-Environment Interaction as a Determinant of Labor Length Variables." *Health Care for Woman International* 7(1986): 341–356.

11. Hodnett, E.D., and Osborn, R. "Effect of Continuous Intrapartum Professional Support on Childbirth Outcomes." *Research in Nursing & Health* 12(1989):289–297.

12. Hofmeyer, G.J.; Nikodem, V.C.; Wolman, W.L. "Companionship to Modify the Clinical Birth Environment: Effects on Progress and Perceptions of Labour and Breast Feeding." *British Journal of Obstetrics and Gynecology* 98(1991):756–764.

13. Keirse, M.J.; Enkin, M.; Lumley, J. "Social and Professional Support during Labor." In *Effective Care in Pregnancy and Childbirth,* vol. 2, edited by I. Chalmers, M. Enkin, and M.J.N.C. Keirse. New York: Oxford University Press, 1989:805–814.

14. Kennell, J.H.; Klaus, M.H.; McGrath, S.K.; Robertson, S.S.; Hinkley, C.W. "Labor Complications Associated with Epidural Anesthesia." *Pediatric Research* 29(1991):220A.

15. Kennell, J.H.; McGrath, S.K.; Klaus, M.H.; Robertson, S.S.; Hinkley, C.W. Response to letter to editor. *Journal of the American Medical Association* 266(1991): 1509–1510.

16. Kennell, J.H.; DeChateau, P.; Wasz-Höckert. John Lind Memorial Symposium. *Infant Mental Health Journal* 8(1987):190–209.

17. Kennell, J.H.; Klaus, M.H.; McGrath, S.K.; Robertson, S.S.; Hinkley, C.W. "Continuous Emotional Support during Labor in a U.S. Hospital." *Journal of the American Medical Association* 265(1991):2197–2201.

18. Kitzinger, S. *The Complete Book of Pregnancy and Childbirth.* New York: Knopf, 1989.

19. Klaus, M.H.; Kennell, J.H.; Robertson, S.S.; Sosa, R. "Effects of Social Support during Parturition on Maternal and Infant Morbidity." *BMJ.* 293(1986):585–587.

20. Klaus, M.H., and Klaus, P. *The Amazing Newborn.* Reading, Mass.: Addison-Wesley/Lawrence, 1985.

21. Klaus, M.H.; Kennell, J.H.; Berkowitz, G.; Klaus, P. "Maternal Assistance and Support in Labor: Father, Nurse, Midwife or Doula?" *Clinical Consultations in Obstetrics and Gynecology* 4 (December 1992).

22. Klaus, M.H., and Kennell, J.H. *Parent-Infant Bonding.* St. Louis: C.V. Mosby, 1982.

23. Lederman, R.P.; Lederman, E.; Work, B.A.; McCann, D.S. "The Relationship of Maternal Anxiety, Plasma Catecholamines, and Plasma Cortisol to Progress in Labor." *American Journal of Obstetrics and Gynecology* 132(1978):495–500.

24. Lederman, R.P.; Lederman, E.; Work, B.A., Jr.; McCann, D.S. "Anxiety and Epinephrine in Multiparous Women in Labor: Relationship to Duration of Labor and Fetal Heart Rate Pattern." *American Journal of Obstetrics and Gynecology* 153(1985):870–877.

25. Lozoff, B.; Jordan, B.; Malone, S. "Childbirth in Cross-cultural Perspective." *Marriage and Family Review* 12(1988):35–60.

26. MacArthur, C.; Lewis, M.; Knox, E.G.; Crawford, J.S. "Epidural Anesthesia and Long-term Backache after Childbirth." *BMJ* 301(1990):9–12.

27. Murray, A.D.; Dolby, R.M.; Nation, R.L.; Thomas, D.B. "Effects of Epidural Anesthesia on Newborns and Their Mothers." *Child Development* 52(1981):71–82.

28. Murray, L., and Carothers, A.D. "The Validation of the Edinburgh Post-natal Depression Scale on a Community Scale." *British Journal of Psychiatry* 157(1990):288–290.

29. Newton, N., and Newton, M. "Mothers' Reactions to Their Newborn Babies." *Journal of the American Medical Association* 181(1962):206–210.

30. Odent, M. *Birth Reborn.* New York: Pantheon Books, 1984.

31. O'Driscoll, K., and Meagher, D. *Active Management of Labor.* 2d ed. London: Bailliere Tindall, 1986.

32. Perez, P., and Snedeker, C. *Special Women: The Role of the Professional Labor Assistant.* Seattle, Wash.: Pennypress, Inc., 1990.

33. Raphael, D. *The Tender Gift: Breastfeeding.* Englewood Cliffs, N.J.: Prentice-Hall, 1973.

34. Scott, J.R., and Rose, N.B. "Effect of Psychoprophylaxis (Lamaze Preparation) on Labor and Delivery in Primaparous." *New England Journal of Medicine* 294(1976): 1205–1207.

35. Simkin, P. *The Birth Partner.* Boston, Mass.: Harvard Common Press, 1989.

36. Sosa, R.; Kennell, J.H.; Robertson, S.; Urrutia, J. "The Effect of a Supportive Companion on Perinatal Problems, Length of Labor and Mother-Infant Interaction." *New England Journal of Medicine* 303(1980):597–600.

37. Thoman, E.B. "Parent-Infant Interaction: How a Rejecting Baby Affects Mother-Infant Synchrony." Ciba Foundation Symposium 33(1975):177–260.

38. Thorp, J.A.; Parisi, V.M.; Boylan, P.C.; Johnston, D.A. "The Effect of Continuous Epidural Analgesia on Cesarean Section for Dystocia in Nulliparous Women." *American Journal of Obstetrics and Gynecology* 162(1989):670–675.

39. Winnicott, D.W. "Primary Maternal Preoccupation." In *Through Paediatrics to Psycho-Analysis.* New York: Basic Books, 1958.

40. Winnicott, D.W. *Babies and Their Mothers.* Reading, Mass.: Addison-Wesley/ Lawrence, 1987.

41. Wolman, W.L. *Social Support during Childbirth: Psychological and Physiological Outcomes.* Master's thesis, University of Witwatersrand, Johannesburg, 1991.

42. Zuspan, F.P.; Cibils, L.A.; Pose, S.V. "Myometrial and Cardiovascular Responses to Alterations in Plasma Epinephrine." *American Journal of Obstetrics and Gynecology* 84(1962):841–851.

INDEX

· · ·
ABOUT THE AUTHORS

MARSHALL H. KLAUS, M.D., is Adjunct Professor of Pediatrics at the University of California, San Francisco and Director of Academic Affairs at the Children's Hospital, Oakland. A distinguished neonatologist and researcher, he is the author or co-author of several standard works in the field, including *Maternal-Infant Bonding, Parent-Infant Bonding, Care of the High-Risk Infant, The Amazing Newborn,* and an editor of the *Yearbook of Neonatal and Perinatal Medicine.*

JOHN H. KENNELL, M.D., is Professor of Pediatrics at Case Western Reserve University School of Medicine and Chief of the Division of Child Development at Rainbow Babies and Children's Hospital in Cleveland, Ohio. In addition to his ongoing research on the doula, his teaching and patient care, he continues to participate each year with first-year medical students who serve as apprentice-physician doulas for mothers. He is the co-author of *Maternal-Infant Bonding* and *Parent-Infant Bonding.*

PHYLLIS H. KLAUS, M.Ed., C.S.W., formerly on the faculty of the Department of Family Practice, Michigan State University, now teaches and practices at the Erickson Institute in Santa Rosa and Berkeley, California, providing psycho- therapy and especially working with the concerns of pregnancy, birth, and the postpartum period. She consults nationally and internationally, does research, and is co-author of *The Amazing Newborn.*